The Wrong Avocado

A gentle guide to easing the emotional journey through cancer

Emma R McNally

Published by Emma R McNally
Edited by Charlotte Noon
Text copyright © Emma R McNally, 2025

The author has made every effort to acknowledge all copyrighted and
trademarked materials. References and links were accurate at the time
of publication; however, their availability, relevance, or appropriateness
cannot be guaranteed. If you notice any errors or omissions, please
report them directly to the author. Where appropriate, corrections will
be made in future editions.

ISBN - 13: 979-8-3527332-3-3

DEDICATION

This book is dedicated to Shaun, my soul mate.
Thank you ... I love you.

iv

CONTENTS

ACKNOWLEDGEMENTS

A heartfelt thank you to my husband, Shaun, for his unwavering love and support during this time, and to my Mum, for her love and always being there when I need her!

To my family and friends, your kindness and encouragement have been a true source of comfort - I am deeply grateful for your outpouring of love and support.

I also want to acknowledge Richard Bandler and John Grinder, the brilliant minds behind NLP (Neuro Linguistic Programming). Their curiosity and pioneering work have made such a difference, and I know this journey would have been far more challenging without NLP.

A special thank you to Charlotte Noon, my wonderful editor, whose expertise and dedication helped bring this book to life, to Esther Taylor, who kindly wrote the foreword and to Ross Willsher for his beautiful photography.

FOREWORD

As CEO of a local breast cancer charity, I have witnessed firsthand how breast cancer is a deeply personal and often overwhelming experience - physically, emotionally, and psychologically. But what I have come to understand, and what this book so gently and powerfully explores, is that while we may not have control over a diagnosis, we do have the ability to shape how we experience the journey.

Emma provides us with an honest and raw account of her own breast cancer journey, from diagnosis to treatment and her recovery. Throughout the book, she offers us a set of tools and techniques that help us understand the language of our own minds - how we think, how we speak to ourselves, and how we make sense of the world around us. For women (and men) navigating the many stages of breast cancer - whether newly diagnosed, in treatment, or moving into life beyond cancer - this can be transformational.

This book will be a vital companion for anyone seeking not just to survive, but to feel more whole, more grounded, and more in control through one of life's toughest journeys. It is practical, compassionate, and filled with wisdom.

May it help you find strength in your thoughts, peace in your heart, and clarity in your path forward.

Esther Taylor

CEO, Lady McAdden Breast Cancer Trust

X

INTRODUCTION

Hello and welcome

My name is Emma, and I have written this book just for you.

As I sit here at my laptop, just two and a half weeks after breast cancer surgery, I feel compelled to share something that may help you.

This morning, I was expecting my post-surgery results, only to learn they haven't arrived yet - I now have another week to wait.

I know that a week may not seem long, but when it feels like your entire life and business depend on these results and the clarity they will bring for the next steps, the wait can be incredibly challenging. Emotionally, it's anything but easy to process.

Since my surgery, I've been toying with the idea of writing something, as Neuro Linguistic Programming (NLP) has been an essential part of my journey. Running an NLP training company, I've used these techniques every single day - honestly, it feels like every single moment, day and night - since the very first hint of my diagnosis.

If you've been through something similar, you probably know what I mean by a 'hint' - when medical professionals subtly (or not so subtly) indicate that cancer is a possibility, even before biopsy results come in. Or perhaps you sensed that something wasn't quite right, long before any official confirmation.

NLP has been invaluable to me during this time and I don't know where I'd be without these tools and insights. They've helped me navigate the toughest and darkest moments - allowing me to feel more resourceful and resilient, understand my emotions on a deeper level, and, when I was ready, shift how I was feeling.

Through this time, I learnt to be kinder to myself and used NLP to rewrite the narrative around cancer, so that my family history didn't have to dictate my future.

What is NLP?

NLP is a practical approach to understanding how our thoughts, language, and behaviour are connected. It offers simple yet powerful tools to help us change unhelpful patterns, manage emotions, and build a more resourceful mindset - especially in times of challenge and uncertainty.

I first discovered NLP around fifteen years ago, and it has been a vital part of my life ever since. I often liken it to fitting a brand-new set of tyres on a car - plus a spare, just in case. It helps you move through life with more ease: giving you better grip during challenging moments, improving your performance, and making the ride altogether smoother.

Over the years, NLP supported me through everyday ups and downs. It helped me navigate the difficult days and savour the joyful ones even more fully. Then came a moment that changed everything: I was told I had cancer. In that instant, it felt as though one of those tyres had been punctured - or more truthfully, like a wheel had fallen off!

In that moment, I knew I had a choice. I could use the NLP tools I had come to trust - to test them in the most personal and profound way - or I could crumble. I chose to use the tools that had already made such a difference in my life to help me through this next phase.

Now, it isn't magic - I absolutely wish it were. However, what NLP did give me was choice. It helped me feel more in control as I continued to live by the principles and gradually started to rebuild my life. I honestly believe that without these tools, the journey would have been far harder - and that's exactly why I feel so passionate about sharing them with you.

NLP was developed in the 1970s by John Grinder and Richard Bandler. They studied experts in therapy and communication - like Milton Erickson, Virginia Satir, and Fritz Perls - and identified the patterns that made them so effective. By modelling their language and behaviour, they discovered that they could achieve similar results. This approach of observing what works and asking, 'How can I do that too?' is at the heart of NLP.

The name itself can be broken down as follows:

- **Neuro** refers to our nervous system - how we think, feel, and process the world.

- **Linguistic** covers all the ways we communicate - words, tone, body language, and even our internal self-talk.

- **Programming** is about recognising and reshaping patterns of behaviour and beliefs that no longer serve us.

Put simply, NLP helps us understand how we create our version of reality and how we can change it, if we choose to. It gives us practical tools to shift thoughts, feelings, and actions, so we can live more purposefully and powerfully.

As Robert Dilts (one of the greats in the NLP field) beautifully put it, NLP is 'the study of the structure of subjective experience'. It helps us make sense of how we experience the world and gives us the tools to shape that experience in ways that truly support us.

What I love most about NLP is that it's not just theory - it's deeply practical. It offers gentle, effective ways to create real change, both personally and professionally.

In my book *Who's Flying Your Plane? How to master the controls of your life* I explore the principles of NLP in more depth - if you're curious, I invite you to take a look.

So here it is - a guide, if you choose to use it - on how to navigate this time in your life. I'll share the tools that helped me through both the darkest moments and the brighter ones, in the hope that something within these pages brings you comfort and makes your own journey a little easier.

Perhaps you are reading this because a loved one is going through cancer or other challenging health conditions. Throughout these pages, I share my experiences - how I felt and what helped me. While your loved one's journey may be different, I hope this insight offers you a deeper understanding and gives you ways to support them, as well as yourself. Feel free to use these tools too (see Chapter 17). I know firsthand that watching someone go through cancer is incredibly difficult. Having greater understanding, deeper empathy, and the ability to manage your own emotions can make a real difference - for both you and them.

Everyone's journey is unique - some things may feel easier, while others are more challenging. There is no right or wrong way to navigate this; after all, it is your journey.

My experience may be different from yours; however, I hope that some of what I share will help you along the way. Most importantly, be kind and gentle with yourself. On the days when you feel good, embrace and enjoy them. And on the less than easy days, I encourage you to explore the tools in this book - they are there to help you move through those moments with greater ease.

How to use this book

It should be noted that this book is intended for educational purposes only. NLP is not a substitute for professional medical advice or treatment. If you have any medical concerns, it is recommended that you seek guidance from a qualified healthcare professional.

If you're listening to the audio version or joining in with the activities, just make sure you're somewhere safe and able to give them your full attention - so, not while driving or operating machinery.

This book is designed to be used however it suits *you*.

You might want to:

- Go straight to the tools in Chapter 17.

- Dip into the chapters that speak to what you are going through right now.

- Or, read it cover to cover, taking in the journey from start to finish.

There are fifty tips scattered throughout - little reminders and insights to support you along the way. You might flick through and see which one catches your eye or revisit them as you need.

Because of this flexible approach, you may notice that some key ideas are revisited in different places. That's intentional - to gently reinforce concepts that are worth coming back to from different angles.

I wish you peace, healing, and hope.

Remember - you've got this ... you are stronger than you think and more incredible than you can ever imagine.

CHAPTER 1 - DEALING WITH THE DIAGNOSIS

If you are anything like me, my diagnosis really knocked me off balance. I had just turned 50 and was enjoying life - running a successful business, getting through the challenges of the Covid pandemic, and beginning to check off the 50 things I'd planned to do for my 50th birthday - when the curveball hit.

I went for my first mammogram, then took a week-long holiday. Upon returning, I found a letter waiting for me. It said there was something unusual, though it could have been an error - or maybe something more. Since I had missed the appointment while away, I called and scheduled another one for the following week, which included a second mammogram, ultrasound, and potentially a biopsy.

After the double biopsy, they told me they suspected it might be cancer. I could hardly believe what I was hearing.

I was at the appointment alone - my husband had gone back to work, as we hadn't expected to get any news that day.

I went straight back to work afterwards, with a full schedule of clients that afternoon. And then, I had to wait a week for the results ... one of the longest weeks of my life.

A week later, the results confirmed that I had two areas of cancer in my right breast. The implications and decisions that followed were anything but easy.

They asked if I had any questions as I faced the decision between a double lumpectomy or a mastectomy - what a decision to make. I left the hospital with a stack of information and the weight of a life-changing choice to consider.

Telling people

I found it helpful to talk to people about my experience, though I understand that this isn't right for everyone. A friend of mine chose to tell no one except her close family.

There's no right or wrong when it comes to what you decide.

Take a moment to think about who you share your news with. Make sure the people you tell will be supportive, encouraging, and uplifting. Right now, it's all about what you need. If you tell many people and they either need your support or share negative stories, it may not be helpful for your mental well-being.

Throughout this journey, your mental strength is incredibly important, so make sure you protect it. I cover this in greater depth in Chapter 7.

It's amazing how everyone suddenly becomes an expert - sharing stories, tips, and 'what I would do' advice. They all mean well, and some of this information can be really helpful. My advice is to consider whether the information is useful to you. If it is, great! If not, simply thank them kindly and let it wash over you.

Protecting your energy

Remember to protect yourself from unhelpful information and people. If someone isn't being supportive, it's okay to limit your time with them (they may be trying their best, but they might say the wrong thing). At this stage, your mind is just as important as your body. Keeping your thoughts positive (more on this later) and limiting negativity around you will support your well-being now and in the future.

If you've noticed that you've absorbed other people's negative energy, take a look at Chapter 17 for ways to clear any unwanted energy. After all, you already have enough of your own to process without taking on others' too! This time is all about you and your healing. That doesn't mean you don't care for others and it's important to give yourself equal, if not greater, care. It's a challenging time, and you deserve to prioritise your well-being.

The first few days after the diagnosis are really the time to be kind to yourself. Ask yourself, 'What do I need right now?' Do you need to talk? Do you need time away from work? Whatever it is, find a way to meet that need. I know some people throw themselves into work, while others take time off. For me, I needed to fulfil my work commitments. My practical, 'get organised' side kicked in, and I focused on rearranging courses and contacting clients. I knew that once I had that all sorted, I could fully focus on healing and preparing myself mentally for the surgery.

Language

Let's talk about the word 'cancer'. If you are like me that word comes with many unhelpful neurological connections. When someone says 'cancer', it triggers an automatic emotional response in your mind - usually fear. This happens because, over the years, through social media, the news, and personal experiences with friends and family, we've formed an association that links cancer with negative beliefs. In my case, I've lost my dad, aunt, grandparents, great aunts, uncles, and step-grandmother to cancer. So, I decided early on that I needed to change my response to the word cancer. It wasn't helpful to carry all those negative associations with my own diagnosis.

At first, I found it helpful to refer to my diagnosis in a more disassociated way. For example, I would say, 'they've given a diagnosis of cancer'. Language is incredibly powerful - neuroscience has shown that words aren't just words. They trigger unique neurological networks in your brain. When we say something repeatedly, especially if it has negative connotations, it strengthens those neural connections every time we access them.

The challenge with this is that when we hear or say the word cancer, we automatically feel bad, which affects our physiology and, in turn, our immune system. On the flip side, positive words follow the same process, and they have a much more beneficial impact on us.

When we say, 'I have cancer', it triggers those unwanted neural pathways and reinforces the negative associations. So, instead, I chose to stay disassociated by using the phrase, 'They say I have cancer'. This helped me avoid embedding the situation even further into my neurology.

Another thing to consider is how people talk about 'fighting' cancer. As you now know, words have a powerful impact on your neurology, and in this context, 'fighting' can be a less-than-positive word. Fighting suggests conflict, and your body is already going through enough internal conflict without adding more battles! Instead, it can be more helpful to think of the cancer cells melting away or rejuvenating into healthy cells, rather than framing it as an internal battle.

One thing to consider is whether you want to take on the cancer label and let it define you. Personally, I know that I am so much more than this temporary blip in my life. And you are too.

Think about all the incredible qualities that make you who you are - your kindness, strength, humour, resilience. Cancer is just one small part of your journey; it doesn't have to become your whole identity. A dear friend once said to me, 'Our bodies are made up of trillions of cells - cancer just means that a few of them have gone a bit wrong, not all of them.' That perspective really helped me.

It reminded me that I am still *me*, and I wasn't going to let this define me or my life.

Now, that doesn't mean I ignored it. I had the treatment I needed, took care of myself, and did everything I could to support my recovery. I chose to see cancer as something that was *temporarily* residing in me - *not* as something that owned me.

The problem with attaching too strongly to the label is that it can feel like cancer is taking over, like it's somehow bigger than *you*. But it isn't. *You* are still here. *You* are still you. And cancer doesn't get to define *you*.

Another challenge that can come with a cancer diagnosis is the feeling that we've lost our sense of identity - like we're no longer *just* ourselves, but instead, this new label has been placed on us. And once that happens, people may start treating us differently.

It's not that they mean to; often, they simply don't know what to say. They are doing their best and they are probably feeling just as uncertain and out of their depth as we are. That's understandable. Fear can make people act awkwardly or say the wrong things.

One thing we *can* control is how we see ourselves. It's so important that we don't fall into the mindset of being a victim (we'll talk more about the 'Why me?' question later). When we see ourselves as victims, it can feel like everything is happening *to* us, leaving us powerless to make changes. The truth is, we *do* have choices. We *do* have strength. And even in the toughest moments, we are still *us* - not just a diagnosis.

Let me be totally open with you - some of what happens along this journey won't be in your control. I mean, let's be honest, none of us *chose* to get cancer! But what truly matters is what we *do* about it.

Do we see ourselves as powerless victims, at the mercy of this disease with no choices or way forward? Or do we recognise that, while we may not have chosen cancer, we *do* have choices - choices about our treatment, our mindset, and most importantly, how we respond to it.

And that's exactly why I'm writing this book. Because while we can't always control what happens, we *can* learn to control how we act, how we think, and what we say about it. That's where our power lies.

Now, I won't pretend it's always easy - it's not. But, knowing that I have some influence over my future and my response gives me strength. I'd rather take ownership of what I can control than hand over my entire future to cancer.

After your diagnosis, my advice is to give yourself the time and space to process it in a way that feels right *for you*. There's no right or wrong way to feel - this is *your* journey, and it's okay to take it at your own pace.

Chances are, you will experience a rollercoaster of emotions - and that leads us perfectly into my next topic ... *emotions!*

#1 Tip

Everyone has an opinion; however, at the end of the day, it's *your* body.

You are the one who needs to make the decision and feel comfortable with the treatment you choose.

#2 Tip

It's completely okay to change your mind.

As the weeks turned into months, I found that my feelings about surgery and treatment evolved.

#3 Tip

Don't google it!

Wait for the professional advice from your surgeon or specialist, as there are plenty of horror stories and misinformation out there.

#4 Tip

Take a moment to consider how you talk about cancer.

You might want to focus on thinking about your body healing and your tumours shrinking, rather than framing it as a fight.

#5 Tip

You are not defined by cancer.

You are a whole, incredible person with amazing qualities and strengths that go far beyond any label - whether it's one you give yourself or one other people place on you.

Take some time to reflect on what truly makes you *you*. What are your strengths, your passions, the qualities that people and you, love about you?

Cancer is just one part of your story - it doesn't get to be the whole thing.

#6 Tip

Even in the midst of this challenge, remember - you *still* have control over your thoughts, emotions, and how you respond to the situation.

That power makes a real difference to how you feel day to day, as well as to your recovery and overall well-being.

Your mindset matters, and I'll be sharing tools later to help you navigate this in a way that supports *you*.

CHAPTER 2 - YOU ARE ALLOWED TO CRY!

When I went in for my double biopsy, I didn't know exactly what was going to happen. I knew my mammogram didn't look right, and I'd been told they might need to do a biopsy. However, I wasn't prepared for what came next. They were able to do one biopsy easily but the other ... well, that required a whole team of people working for 90 minutes just to get the samples they needed.

It was extremely uncomfortable, to say the least. At one point, I was bent over backwards, lying down with the machine pressing on my existing biopsy site as they asked me to stay still while they went off to x-ray the samples. In that moment, my sense of dignity had long left the room, and my sense of calm was slipping away too. I knew if I panicked or allowed myself to become stressed, it would only make things worse. I had no choice but to stay calm.

So, I closed my eyes, focused on accessing states of calm, peace, and tranquillity, and blocked my mind from the pain. I just lay there, waiting. Of course, it wasn't pleasant, but it would have been far worse if I hadn't known how to manage my state of mind.

This can be an incredibly emotional time. It's normal to experience waves of anxiety while waiting for results, and once you receive them, there's a whole new layer of processing to go through. It's completely natural to feel a mix of emotions - there's a lot to take in, and it's okay to give yourself the time and space to do that.

My background is in change management, and I've often used Kübler-Ross's Change Curve to explain how we process emotions during significant life changes. The emotions - shock, denial, frustration, anger, and depression - occur naturally before gradually moving toward acceptance and problem-solving.

You won't necessarily experience them in a neat, linear order. In fact, it's completely normal to cycle through them multiple times in a random order. The key is recognising where you are and knowing that these emotions are part of the journey.

When I found myself stuck in one of these stages and struggling to move forward, I turned to NLP. It's been incredibly helpful in shifting my mindset and regaining a sense of control

To truly start moving forward, I found that I needed to reach a place of acceptance. It took me a little while to get my head around, but I came to realise that acceptance isn't about giving in - it's about acknowledging what is.

Michael Hall, in his book *Resilience: Being the Phoenix* (2020, p43), explains that acceptance is not the same as tolerance, resignation, condoning, or approving. Instead: 'Acceptance means acknowledging current reality for what it is.' Because if we don't accept what's happening, we can't take meaningful action to change or respond to it.

This shift in perspective made all the difference - it allowed me to stop fighting against reality and start working *with* it and *through* it.

When it comes to cancer, there are a few additional emotions that can come up, like fear, anxiety, and worry. The level of uncertainty can be overwhelming - you are not sure what's happening, you are waiting for results, and even once you have the next steps, there's still that nagging 'what if?' and the tendency to catastrophise.

The good news is that, with a little practice, we can start to realise that we have control over what's happening in our minds. Our emotions don't have to control us. We can learn to manage them more easily, and even when something feels completely out of our control, we can still find a way to shift how we feel for the better - if we choose to.

That's what NLP is all about: giving us choices, rather than letting us be at the mercy of events.

It's important to remember that it's okay to cry. After all, crying can help release and process the emotions we're holding inside. There were definitely moments when I cried.

One emotion that really caught me by surprise was grief - the grief of potentially losing part of my body. I know it may sound strange or even shallow but when you are emotionally and physically attached to something, it can be incredibly difficult to imagine losing it. This can be tied to your identity, your self-image, and so much more.

For me, it really hit a couple of weeks before my operation. We had a planned holiday, and I was having a wonderful time. One day, I put on a new bikini and realised that this could be the last time I'd sunbathe with the body I had. Now, don't get me wrong, I'm not saying my figure is anything extraordinary, but it's *my* body - the only one I have - and I'm quite attached to it!

The thought of losing part of me was really upsetting, and the tears flowed - uncontrollably - for a good hour or more.

And then, when I felt I'd released everything I needed to, I chose to stop. I let it all out, and then I moved on.

This is one way to process things - there are others.

Any emotions you are experiencing are completely natural. It's not about labelling them as good or bad - it's more about whether they are helpful or not. I once worked with someone who couldn't stop crying before a scan. She came to me because she wanted to overcome the anxiety and stop the tears, as they weren't helping her at that moment.

So, if you are finding that a particular emotion keeps coming up and you want to shift it, take a look at Chapter 17. I share a powerful technique that can help you collapse that unwanted emotion and move forward with more ease.

Emotions, like pain, are signals that something isn't quite right. Rather than simply changing or blocking these emotions, it's important to understand what they are trying to communicate. I know that if I overdo things, I'll experience pain - this is my body's way of signalling me to stop. Similarly, if I feel an unwanted emotion, it's a sign that something needs attention, and I need to understand the positive message behind it before I let it go.

This idea of a 'positive intention' is key. For example, fear, worry, and anxiety often signal that we perceive something as unsafe, indicating a need for protection. When we experience these emotions, the amygdala in our brain becomes active, triggering the fight, flight, or freeze stress response - originally designed to protect us from physical dangers, such as sabre-toothed tigers.

In today's world, though, our unconscious mind can sometimes get confused, thinking we're facing physical danger even when we're not. Cancer can feel like a sabre-toothed tiger, and so fear, anxiety, and worry may feel like natural responses.

The problem is that when we feel these emotions regularly, it's like all the fire alarms in a building are going off at once, and we don't know where the fire is. Or it's like driving your car while riding the clutch - at some point, everything will burn out.

So yes, there is a positive intention behind these emotions - for example, to keep us safe. However, when we experience them too often, they don't serve us in the long run. When a real threat arises, we might not notice it because we've been so overwhelmed by the constant alarms.

It's completely natural to feel fear, anxiety, and worry; however, when these emotions persist for extended periods, they don't just become unhelpful - they also affect us physically. Research in psychoneuroimmunology has shown a direct link between our emotional state and our physical health, particularly the functioning of our immune system.

So, while fear and anxiety have their purpose, it's far more beneficial to feel calm and resourceful, rather than stressed, anxious, fearful, or worried. Those emotions don't help us - they can actually be detrimental to our health, and we need the best health we can possibly have during this time.

If you are finding that you are constantly feeling these emotions, it could have an impact on your recovery. The situation itself is going to be the same - whether you face it with fear and anxiety or with calm and peace. I know it might sound a bit fatalistic but, in my experience, I was going to have the operation either way. I could choose to face it feeling calm, resourceful, and peaceful, or I could choose to face it feeling anxious, worried, and fearful. Knowing what I know, I chose the former (calm, resourceful, and peaceful) because I knew it would support my recovery and help me feel better about the whole situation.

That sounds great, I hear you say, but how can we actually do this? Well, the answer lies in the science of neuroplasticity - the brain's ability to change and adapt. Have you ever noticed how the more you practise something, the easier it gets? Even if it's just eating chocolate in front of the TV! This is how we create habits and learn new things: by repeating something over and over in our minds, we strengthen neurological pathways over time.

In the same way, we can create new triggers that fire off more positive emotional pathways. This is called 'anchoring', and it works through a process known as 'classic conditioning'. Over time, neurons become 'wired together' - in other words, messages are sent down those neural pathways again and again, so when the trigger is activated, you get the same response.

This concept was famously demonstrated by Pavlov with his dogs. He found that when he presented food, the dogs would salivate. Then, he rang a bell at the same time as presenting the food. After repeating this several times, he rang the bell *without* the food - and the dogs still salivated.

This neurological connection is the same when you hear a song that takes you back to an amazing time, and you instantly feel great, or when you see a picture of a previous holiday and feel relaxed and calm. We can apply this naturally occurring phenomenon *deliberately* to create new, resourceful states for ourselves - states like peace or calm.

For more details on how to create these new resources, check out the tools section (Chapter 17). You can also use similar techniques to collapse out unwanted emotions, like fear, so that you can feel more resourceful and in control.

Before my operation, I created a resource anchor that included flexibility (since I wasn't sure what to expect, I figured I might need to stay flexible), as well as confidence, calmness, peace, and feeling grounded. I used this anchor throughout the day of my operation - when I was having wires inserted (which was very uncomfortable), when I spent 8 hours waiting for the operation, and even when I was taken down to the operating theatre.

Note: A resource anchor is basically a shortcut your brain can use to help you feel better - and it's all thanks to something called neuroplasticity (your brain's amazing ability to create new patterns). It's a bit like how you feel when you hug a friend - your mood lifts instantly. That's a natural anchor. With NLP, you can create your own version of this. For example, you might press your knuckle while feeling calm, strong or happy. Then, later, just pressing your knuckle can bring that feeling back. It gives you a way to shift how you feel without needing something specific to happen first. You get to choose your state. See Chapter 17 for guidance as to how to create a resource anchor for yourself.

You can use these tools anytime you are going through something difficult - or, in fact, anytime in the future. They are incredibly useful to have up your sleeve.

However, sometimes we may actually want to feel certain emotions, and that's okay too. It's just important to have tools at your disposal to change them if you feel stuck or want to shift your emotional state. Having these tools gives you the opportunity to choose, rather than feeling at the mercy of your situation.

You can use these tools to shift any emotions that aren't working for you, or to create new resource anchors for emotions you want to experience more of. But what if you don't know how you are supposed to feel? That's totally okay too. Sometimes we feel like we *should* feel a certain way, or we just feel numb - and that's all completely normal.

Remember to be kind to yourself - there's no right or wrong way to feel.

It's your journey, not someone else's. Just because someone else is worried, or thinks you should be, doesn't mean you have to feel that way. Take the time you need in whatever way works best for you to help you feel better - whether that's chatting with a friend, meditating, watching a movie, going for a walk or something else. All of these things can help.

Sometimes, we just need time to process what's happening, or you may feel lost - unsure of your way. This is perfectly natural, as this can be such a time of uncertainty. Often, all we can see is the situation around us: our diagnosis, our treatment. Everywhere we look, it seems to be about cancer and what's happening. It's not unusual to feel like we've lost our sense of self (remember, you are so much more than your diagnosis).

It's also important to remember that you can start thinking about what you want to do and the experiences you want to have, beyond your treatment. I know it can feel all-consuming but there is so much more out there for all of us, no matter what our diagnosis may be.

I remember when I first got my diagnosis, I had to cancel and rearrange work. This was something I had never done before, and it felt awful. I love what I do, and giving people the tools to help themselves and others is my passion. At that time, I wasn't sure what my treatment would be or how long my recovery would take.

At one point, I considered cancelling a course I had scheduled for the autumn (since my operation was in mid-August). However, the thought of not having something to look forward to wasn't good for me. If I needed to cancel closer to the time, so be it! Without something in my future to look forward to, I felt it would be tough psychologically.

So, what do you have to look forward to? It could be a walk on the beach, a meal with loved ones, time in nature, holding the hand of a friend, or even a holiday. It doesn't matter how big or small - it's important to have some fun things on the calendar. You can always move them if you need to. Having something to look forward to in the future can really help guide you through the tougher times.

#7 Tip

Notice how you are feeling and ask yourself: Is this emotion useful, helpful, and kind?

If not, then take action to collapse it out so you can feel more resourceful.

Check out the Collapsing Anchor technique in Chapter 17.

#8 Tip

We can choose how we feel, if we want to.

By using neuroplasticity, we can create resource anchors that we can rely on at any time - especially during those less-than-easy moments, like when you are going through treatment or waiting for surgery.

#9 Tip

However you feel (even if you don't know how you feel or think you should feel), that's totally fine.

Be kind to yourself and remember that you can always choose to change how you want to feel, if you wish to.

#10 Tip

Start thinking about the experiences and fun things you want to do during or after your treatment.

Having something to look forward to can make a big difference in your mindset and help guide you through the tougher times.

CHAPTER 3 - CHANGING THE NARRATIVE

As mentioned before, the word 'cancer' can trigger all sorts of emotional reactions, shaped by your personal experiences, the media, news, research, and others' opinions. For many, it's not a pleasant feeling, and the narrative - the story we tell ourselves about it and our future - can often be less than helpful.

When I was diagnosed, my first thoughts were, 'Really? That's so early - my dad was at least retired when he first got it at 62 ... I'm only 50!' Unpacking that statement, I realised not only did I have a belief that I was going to get cancer, but I also believed I was likely to eventually die from it - one of my biggest fears. So, I did some work on the fear and beliefs, because they definitely weren't helping me.

As mentioned earlier, what we feel affects us physically as well as mentally, and to recover well, we need to be in the best possible physical and mental state. Even if we're physically in the hands of doctors, we still have the power to choose our mental well-being. Cancer may be a condition of the body, but we must take care not to allow it to infiltrate our thoughts, because that won't help our healing process. I realised that my thoughts were driving my feelings of fear, so I needed to change those thoughts and beliefs - I needed to rewrite my narrative around the situation.

With all the information out there, such as '1 in 2 of us will get cancer' and other similar messages, it's not always easy to shake off those fears. The good news, though, is that many people survive, and one of the most helpful things we can do to aid our recovery and survival is to nurture a positive mental attitude.

Now, you might feel really strong in this area - great! Or maybe you have those nagging doubts that creep in, especially at night - the 'what ifs?' I know when I first found out, I made sure to get my house in order, metaphorically speaking. I checked my will, asked friends to look out for my husband ... just in case. Once I'd done that, I realised it was time to shift my beliefs about what was happening. I needed to change the running commentary in my mind to ensure that what I was telling myself and what I believed would support me through the whole process.

It's tough enough to deal with the physical side of things without adding mental and emotional struggles on top of it.

I worked with a coach to change the beliefs that were holding me back and the doubts I had. I even worked with the cancer to discover what I needed to learn from it being there, so I could give myself the best chance of recovering and prevent it from coming back. Our brains and bodies are truly amazing. For many years, we thought they were separate - that what we thought had no impact on our physical health. However, we now know that isn't the case. We know the mind and body are connected.

If we push ourselves too hard, our bodies send us signals like pain, and it's up to us to listen to what our bodies need. I have to admit, I haven't always been great at this. I used to work non-stop and then wonder why I would get sick every Christmas when I finally stopped! It was my body's way of forcing me to rest because I hadn't been listening to it in the months leading up to that time off.

Our conscious mind is the part that is rational, logical, and responsible for managing our thoughts. Our unconscious mind, on the other hand, is the part that takes care of the blueprint for our health, stores our memories, and holds the answers we need. It's the part we often overlook, especially when it comes to the messages it's trying to send about our health.

This was a crucial time when I knew I needed to reconnect with my unconscious mind. I needed to understand what it was trying to tell me and what I needed in order to get through this challenging time. One of the things I realised was that I needed to change my narrative about cancer and adjust my beliefs around it. This shift in perspective was essential for me to move forward in a more empowered way. If you are interested, check out Chapter 17 for a process that can help you do the same.

Beliefs are incredibly powerful. You've probably heard of the placebo effect, where people take a pill that has no medical properties, yet they feel better after taking it. This phenomenon is well-known, and it's a perfect example of how beliefs can influence our thoughts and actions, as well as our unconscious mind and behaviour. This is where the concept of a self-fulfilling prophecy comes into play.

Beliefs can shift in an instant. We've all experienced this, I'm sure, especially when faced with a life-changing diagnosis. For instance, there I was, feeling amazing, fit, well, and healthy, living my best life and doing my '50 things for 50,' when suddenly I was diagnosed with cancer. That news changed my belief about my health in a heartbeat!

What I realised, however, is that the next part of my recovery wasn't solely in the hands of my surgeon. It was also in *my* hands, through my beliefs and mental resilience. I had a choice: I could crumble under the weight of my diagnosis (and trust me, it would have been easy to do so) and adopt the belief that cancer defines me, or I could choose to believe that I would recover, heal, and survive.

I just want to take a moment to talk about what a belief really is. Essentially, a belief can be defined as a 'truism for you'. Notice that it's *for you*, not for anyone else, but for *you*. So, what do you want to believe?

I wanted to believe that my cancers were shrinking and disappearing. Did the evidence support that? Not exactly but I needed to believe it because I knew it was the healthiest mindset I could adopt to keep myself mentally strong during such a challenging time. I chose to follow the medical advice and go ahead with the operation; however, every day I visualised my tumours shrinking. I imagined myself as healthy, with my body responding in a great way and healing itself.

Whenever doubt crept in, I worked to change it. I knew that if I started to focus on the negative or dwell on the harsh reality of the situation, it would only have a detrimental effect on my mental well-being, and that wouldn't help me. That doesn't mean I ignored the reality

- I still prepared for my operation, but I chose not to let myself spiral down into the negative 'what if' thinking. And if I did start to head in that direction, I would stop myself and choose to think differently.

From the moment I was diagnosed, I chose to believe that my tumours were shrinking and that I was healing. So, when the day of the operation arrived, and they did the ultrasound to place the wires in the right position to guide the surgeon, I had my hopes high that they had shrunk or even disappeared. Unfortunately, the ultrasound showed that the tumours were still there, and the surgery was still necessary.

At that point, I was obviously disappointed, since the evidence didn't align with my positive belief. However, here's the thing: I didn't let that shake me - a slight wobble, yes. However, I had worked on creating an anchor for flexibility (see Chapter 17), which helped me stay grounded and open-minded, even if things didn't go exactly as I had hoped.

I could have chosen to focus on the fear that my tumours were growing inside of me. I could have let that thought spiral, but I knew that would not serve me. Instead, I kept my belief that I was healing, even if the physical evidence didn't match up. And while I'll never know for sure, I honestly believe that staying positive and focused on healing helped me maintain the best mental state possible as I prepared for surgery.

In the end, having that positive mindset didn't just make the waiting period easier; it made me feel like I was in control of my journey. It was about choosing a mindset that supported me, instead of one that could have dragged me down. And that's a choice we all have - we may not always be able to change the physical facts, but we can certainly choose the story we tell ourselves and how we choose to respond. And that can make all the difference.

A friend of mine once asked a powerful question about beliefs: 'Are they useful, supportive, and kind?' If the answer is yes, then that's fantastic! However, if your beliefs are unhelpful, either to you or others, or if they are limiting you in some way, or are unkind, remember that you have the power to change them.

Once you've shifted your beliefs to ones that are more supportive, the next step is to change the language you use. I found that how I spoke about my situation made a huge difference. If I caught myself saying something unhelpful, I would stop and change it. This also applies to how you talk about cancer. Is it something dark, overwhelming, and like an intense battle? What if, instead, we described it as a journey or a bump in the road (perhaps a large bump, but still just a bump!)? Or even as a time for ourselves, a time to learn?

The way we talk to ourselves affects our neurology. Using softer, more positive language sends kinder signals to your brain. Words like 'terminal,' 'severe,' and 'painful' trigger negative neurological responses. However, if you describe things as 'less than easy,' you are activating a more positive and resourceful state of mind. Your brain doesn't process negation - just like when you do an internet search for 'not cancer' you get cancer-related results. So, instead of focusing on what you don't want, speak about what you *do* want.

It may sound like a mind game but it's a game worth playing. Through everything you are going through, the one thing you have control over is your mind. Your body might feel like it's out of your control, but your thoughts? Those are yours to manage. By choosing kinder, more empowering language, you can make the journey a little easier on both your mind and body.

Of course, there were times when doubts crept in - and that's completely normal - that's exactly why I created my resource anchor. It was something I could turn to and use whenever I needed it. Instead of letting the doubts take over, I reminded myself that I had this tool at my disposal. Knowing that I had this anchor gave me the freedom to release those doubts and stay focused on beliefs that were supportive and helpful for me.

I truly believe that your past doesn't have to define your future. And someone else's journey doesn't have to determine your own. This is your journey, and mentally, you are in the driver's seat - you have choice, and nothing can take that away from you. One of my favourite equations is:

Event + Response = Outcome.

The event - such as a diagnosis, treatment, and everything else that comes with it - may or may not be in your control. But how you respond to it is, and your response will have a big impact on the outcome.

One way to change your response as already mentioned, is by shifting any beliefs that aren't serving you. By choosing to think in a different, more supportive way, you can begin to take control of your mental state and approach the situation with a new mindset.

#11 Tip

What is your narrative?

What do you believe about your situation?

What are you saying?

Is it helpful or not?

If not, then you can choose to change it.

See Chapter 17 to find out how.

#12 Tip

Your beliefs and the narrative you create don't always have to be based on what's true right now, but they should always be useful and supportive for you.

It's about choosing a mindset that helps you feel stronger, more empowered, and better equipped to handle whatever comes your way.

It's not about ignoring reality; it's about focusing on what you can control - your thoughts and how you approach each moment.

#13 Tip

Even when the events happening around us feel out of our control, we still have control over how we respond.

And how we respond can greatly influence the outcome.

Remember, it's not what happens to you that matters most; it's what you choose to do about it.

CHAPTER 4 - IT'S A WAITING GAME

For some, everything may feel like it's moving at a rapid pace, while for others, it can seem like time is stretching on forever. Ultimately, it all comes down to perspective.

If your perspective is serving you well, that's fantastic. However, if it's not, and you are finding that your response isn't quite what you would like it to be, the good news is that you have the power to change it. Take, for example, the time when I was waiting for the results of my operation. It was an event outside my control; however, my response to it would make all the difference to how I felt during that week. I could have let myself get frustrated, blamed others, and spiralled into anxiety. Or I could choose to see it as another week of recovery, a chance to get stronger and healthier for the next stages of my treatment. The choice was mine, and it's always yours too.

The meaning we assign to situations has a powerful impact on how we feel about them. For example, when

50

we attach a negative meaning to something, we naturally experience negative emotions - because our feelings are deeply linked to how we are interpreting it. The good news is, we have the power to change the meaning we assign. If you define a situation as 'bad', you will likely feel bad. However, if you change that meaning to something like 'less than easy,' you will start to feel better about it and be able to move forward with more positivity.

In NLP, we use a process called 'reframing' - which is essentially the art of thinking differently. It's not about determining what's right or wrong but rather about figuring out what serves you better. It's about choosing perspectives that help you feel more resourceful and build mental resilience. When I reframed my situation, I was more focused on finding what would empower me and keep me strong, rather than getting stuck in what could have felt overwhelming.

Reframing is all about exploring what else a situation or event could mean. It's incredibly powerful, and I really encourage you to explore different perspectives, especially during this time, so your thoughts can be helpful and supportive. I'd also suggest that you do this for yourself. While others might help to reframe for you, it can be a bit grating if it's not done in a sensitive way. If someone had said, 'Oh well, at least you've got another week to recover,' I probably would have been upset due to a lack of empathy.

Once you've given yourself the space to process what's happening, you can start gently exploring what you want to believe about the situation. In my case, yes, that extra time gave me longer to recover, and it also gave me the opportunity to start writing this book for you.

Reframing is such a powerful tool, and when you use it gently on your own narrative, it can be incredibly helpful - especially when events or situations that impact us are outside of our control.

Reframing is fascinating because we put a frame around everything that happens - it's how we make sense of the world. We have basic frames, like whether something is good or bad, healthy or not, and then we have the more personal frames or lenses through which we see things - all of which are subjective. For example, one person might think a new prime minister is great, while someone else may not feel the same.

What's important here, especially when it comes to your health journey, is that it's not about being right or wrong - it's about whether your perspective is helpful or not. If you view treatment as a negative or unpleasant experience, or if hearing the word cancer triggers unhelpful emotions, then that becomes the lens through which you see the whole situation. And if that's your lens, it can end up being a self-fulfilling prophecy - in other words, your reality becomes a reflection of your expectations. If you are convinced something is going to be 'bad', you will likely start to notice and focus on all the negative parts of the experience.

Just a quick note on the science behind this: we have a part of our brain called the Reticular Activating System (RAS), which helps filter information and directs our attention toward what we focus on. This is why, when you were first diagnosed, it probably felt like all you noticed was cancer, for example, in adverts, on the news, in conversation with friends and so on. It was always there but your brain hadn't previously been tuning into it.

Another example of your RAS at work is when you've just bought a new car. Suddenly, you see that car everywhere - on the road and in adverts. It's not that everyone else has suddenly bought the same car - it's just that your RAS is filtering in what you are now focused on. Your brain has decided this is important to you, so it brings it to your attention more often.

Now, if we approach situations with a more positive mindset, our RAS will start to search for the positives, making it easier for us to navigate the experience. We'll feel more resourceful and better equipped to handle whatever comes our way.

I'm not suggesting we live in denial, but by shifting our thoughts so we don't keep dwelling on the negative can be really helpful for our mental well-being. It's about finding a balance, so we're not constantly projecting worry, but rather looking for ways to feel stronger and more supported through it all.

When we think about a situation that hasn't happened yet, we're essentially creating a story or narrative about how it's going to play out. The key question I ask myself is: is that story helpful or not? For instance, if I start worrying that I won't be able to ask questions or that the news is going to be bad, then I'm stressing over something in advance. However, worry doesn't change the outcome – as Robert Downie Jr says, 'worrying is like praying for what you don't want to happen.'

Instead, I've found it much more useful to prepare: write down my questions, have someone with me at appointments, create a resource anchor, or do whatever else feels appropriate for the situation. Being ready for whatever comes my way and then deciding how I want to think about it, is far more empowering.

Ask yourself: what else could happen that would be more helpful, more supportive, and kinder to myself? This was especially important for me during the waiting periods. It was easy to imagine all sorts of worst-case scenarios, but I chose to focus on the positive and take care of both my mental and physical health.

During the waiting time, I knew I needed to be mindful of what I read and how I spent my time. It was easy to slip into negative thoughts about the outcome and what was happening to me. It was all too easy to feel sorry for myself and become upset. I knew that this wouldn't help me mentally or physically. I had to ensure that I was taking care of my mental well-being. You've probably heard about the power of gratitude, and how it can shift our perspective, thoughts, and emotions to a more positive place.

One particular day of waiting, I had watched a programme on breast cancer, and it was the day after our dear Queen had passed away. I could feel myself becoming tearful and upset - definitely not the best place to be. I still had to do three sets of exercises a day, and my last set was before dinner. I went upstairs to do my exercises, but I knew I needed to shift how I was feeling.

So, I decided to use my exercises as an opportunity to change my focus.

I had to hold stretches for a count of ten, and with each count, I named something I was grateful for - my husband, my surgeon, my home, the breast that was well, the air I was breathing, the clothes I was wearing ... by the end of the exercises, I had listed over 100 things I was grateful for. I felt so different! I came downstairs feeling lighter, brighter, and ready to enjoy the evening with my husband.

The reason why some of us find waiting less than easy is because of the uncertainty around the outcome. When you are waiting for results, the thoughts can start to swirl in your mind (as mentioned before, reframing those thoughts can really help). However, it's also the uncertainty that we need to manage. I found that keeping myself busy with productive activities was key to making sure both my mind and body stayed occupied. One helpful technique is to focus on all the things that are within your control - the things you have certainty over. By holding onto these, you can create a sense of stability and calm during the waiting period.

Uncertainty often makes us feel out of control. It's as if the outcome is in someone else's hands, not our own. It can feel like the world has stopped for us, even though life is carrying on as usual for everyone else. This sense of being on hold can be overwhelming but there are ways to regain a sense of control.

One way is to practise grounding (see Chapter 17), which helps you feel more connected. You can also change your state to one of feeling more in control through techniques like balanced breathing (also in Chapter 17), meditation, or visualisation (see Chapter 18, Additional Support). These methods are all useful for creating a sense of calm.

A quick and easy tool I've used is to make a list of everything I can control. For example, draw around your hand and write all the things that are outside your control on the outside (e.g. the results of the operation, the next steps) and then write everything you can control inside the hand (e.g. what you eat, how much exercise you do, what you wear, the thoughts you have, what you say, what you watch on TV, and how you spend your time). It's amazing how many things we actually have the power to influence. By focusing on these, we can restore a sense of certainty and remind ourselves of what we truly have control over.

This was invaluable for me during my waiting time, and I hope it can help you too.

#14 Tip

Pay attention to how you are interpreting your situation.

Is it helping you?

If not, ask yourself, 'What else could this situation mean?'

No situation or event has any inherent meaning except the one you give it.

The meaning is subjective, and this gives you the power to choose a more helpful interpretation, if you wish.

#15 Tip

Our futures are not yet written - we don't yet know what our futures hold. We may have some idea, but we don't really know for certain.

Therefore, if you are going to make up a narrative, why not make it a good one?

Focus on the positive possibilities rather than worrying about what could go wrong. After all, your mind will create a narrative - so why not choose one that supports and empowers you?

#16 Tip

Notice how you are feeling and use gratitude to shift
your state if you need to.

Gratitude has the power to change your focus, elevate
your mood, and help you regain a positive perspective,
especially when facing difficult moments.

#17 Tip

If you are feeling that things are out of your control or dealing with uncertainty, shift your focus to what you *can* control.

This simple shift can help reduce your stress and calm your mind.

By focusing on what's within your power, you can regain a sense of control and feel more grounded during challenging times.

CHAPTER 5 - WHY ME?

You may find yourself (or others) asking, 'Why me?' It's a natural thought to have but it's not particularly helpful. The truth is, the 'why me?' question doesn't really have an answer, and often, it leads us to a dark and unproductive place.

As Gabor Maté writes in *When the Body Says No*:

> 'None of us are to be blamed if we succumb to illness and death. Any one of us might succumb at any time, but the more we can learn about ourselves, the less prone we are to become passive victims.'

I found it more helpful to ask myself, 'What can I learn from this?' or 'What do I want to do differently because of this?' These questions guide me forward and make it easier to navigate through tough times. What matters most is not what happens to me, but how I respond to it -

how I manage it, how I move forward, and how I can find a way to thrive.

Be gentle with yourself on this one - it's all about timing. The idea that cancer could provide an opportunity for change might be new to you, and it's a pretty big shift in perspective. For me, though, it was a game-changer. I realised that one of the key things I needed to adjust was the hours I was working and the balance in my life. I had already started making changes before cancer, focusing more on what I loved to do outside work (although I do love my work too). It was all about creating a healthier balance.

Cancer really gave me a wake-up call. At 50, I was shocked to find myself facing cancer. It made me realise I had to seize this moment to shape my future in a way that truly felt right for me, rather than just continuing to follow the same old path. I came to the understanding that my main focus going forward needed to be my health and recovery.

Whether there's something to learn or something to change is entirely up to you. Do you want your life to look different? I'm guessing you'd love to not have cancer - I'm right there with you on that! If we look beyond the diagnosis, and take a more grateful view of life, how do we want the next chapter to be?

For me, cancer became a time to reconnect with my true self and appreciate how many wonderful things I have in my life. It gave me the chance to work in a different way - being more present, meditating, reading, learning, writing, socialising, travelling, and spending more time with my family. It also helped me to notice and appreciate the tiny things I had taken for granted.

Yes, cancer is real, and it can feel overwhelming at times, and by shifting the way we view it, it doesn't have to feel as huge or looming. It can actually be a catalyst for change, if that's something you want it to be.

I look back on my life and think about the first 25 years - those were the years of growing up, finding love, and figuring out who I thought I was. The next 25 years were focused on my career, business, and work. And now, I ask myself, what do I want the next 25 years to be? And the 25 after that?

I don't know how long I have on this earth - none of us do. By focusing on both the big and small things we want for the future, we're sending a clear message to our unconscious mind: we want to live, we want to be here, and we want to make a difference.

I know life can feel busy, and sometimes we're rushing from one thing to the next, missing out on truly experiencing life. Cancer gave me the chance to stop - a forced stop - to wake up to my life and ask myself, 'What do I really want?' 'What do I want to learn?'

I've always been someone who loves learning, and now, during my recovery, I've had the chance to dive deeper into it. I spent my time listening to audios, reading books about the brain and neuroscience, and discovering more about how our thoughts can actually help our bodies heal. It's a reminder that even in the toughest of times, there's always something new to learn and ways to grow.

Some people believe that everything happens for a reason. I think the more useful question is: 'What do I want to learn from this in order to move forward?' Our unconscious mind holds a wealth of wisdom - in the form of stored experiences, learned patterns, and intuitive responses - and plays a crucial role in influencing our physical health. Often, we don't listen to our bodies as much as we should - we ignore the need for rest, skip exercise, or indulge in things that aren't beneficial to us. Our bodies are incredibly resilient and put up with a lot - I know mine certainly does.

Sometimes, our unconscious mind sends us little warning signs, subtle hints that something needs to change. If we don't listen to those signs, they can become louder and more persistent until something bigger happens. Could this be the reason for my cancer? Who knows? It could be my lifestyle, stress, the food I eat, or even pollution. There's so much conflicting research out there ... or maybe it's none of these things at all. The truth is, we don't always know why these things happen.

What I found more helpful was to honestly check in with myself to see if there was anything I wanted to do differently - and then actually doing it. Maybe there's a reason for having cancer, maybe not - what does matter however, is what you do moving forward. What matters is how you support yourself, how you show yourself kindness, and how you give yourself the best opportunity to heal and truly live.

Understanding what you need to do to get through the early stages is incredibly helpful. As you start to feel better, giving yourself the space to reflect on your life - what's working for you and whether there's anything you'd like to learn or change - helps you move forward.

When we listen to our unconscious mind and learn how to communicate with it, we can give ourselves the support we need. This is such a powerful place to be. By understanding the lessons in big emotional events, we allow our unconscious mind to store those learnings, making it easier to move on and heal.

As you move forward through this time, learning as you go will help you release some of the unwanted emotions that come with it.

If you find this less than easy, I highly recommend working with an NLP Professional who can guide you through this process and help you turn this time into a catalyst for positive change, rather than allowing it to have a negative emotional impact on your life.

None of us know how much time we have left - whether it's hours, days, months, or years. What matters is making the most of our time on this earth. Even if our bodies aren't where we want them to be physically, we can still create a fulfilling life by training our minds. Use the tools shared in this book to change the way you think, the way you talk to yourself and others, and the way you feel emotionally. This can lead to a richer, more fulfilling life, with or without cancer.

One of the most powerful tools I used during my recovery is visualisation. There's a wealth of research supporting the power of the mind through visualisation, showing that the brain reacts in much the same way when we visualise doing something as it does when we're actually doing it. For example, you can use visualisation for physical activity, and it's also incredibly effective for healing.

This brings me to the tools I used to prepare for surgery which I cover in the next chapter.

#18 Tip

Sometimes, the experience of cancer can open the door
to change ... if and when the moment feels right for you.

#19 Tip

Is there something you'd like to learn from
this experience?

Is there something you want to change or do differently?

Give yourself the space to explore these questions and
reflect on what might be most helpful for you
moving forward.

#20 Tip

Thriving is about mental strength, not just our physical bodies.

Even if you can't swim, walk, or run right now, you can still cultivate mental agility through your thoughts, feelings, and the way you speak.

This mental resilience is incredibly powerful when it comes to your recovery.

CHAPTER 6 - PRE-SURGERY PREPARATION

This is one of the most important times in our journey. At first, I thought the post-surgery phase was the most crucial. However, I soon realised that preparing myself before surgery was just as important to ensure I was in the best possible place to face the operation. Even if you are not having surgery, you can still apply this approach to any treatments or upcoming events where you want to feel more resourceful and ready.

My learning journey began here. Not only did I gain more knowledge about cancer than I ever expected, but I also had to learn what I personally needed to not only get through the operation but to thrive and recover fully. This was where the real thought work began. I dedicated time to examining my beliefs about cancer (see Chapter 3).

Other things may come up during this time that seem completely unrelated to cancer - they certainly did for me.

One of the biggest realisations I had was the feeling that it was too late. At the age of 50 and with cancer, I suddenly realised that opportunities had passed.

The reason I'm sharing this is because, during this time of reflection, something totally unrelated might pop up. After all, receiving a cancer diagnosis is a big wake-up call. I used this as an opportunity to go deep, to let go, to forgive myself for not making a different choice, and to heal. I used a gentle process called Core Transformation (created by Connirae Andreas) to help with this (visit www.achieveyourgreatness.co.uk/core-transformation for more information or coaching support).

So, if other seemingly unrelated thoughts or emotions are coming up for you, know that this is completely natural. It's simply your unconscious mind taking the opportunity to be heard and to begin healing. Give yourself space to acknowledge these feelings with kindness and curiosity - you might just uncover something that brings you even greater clarity and peace.

I also spent a lot of time visualising my body healing. Visualisation isn't just about seeing - it's about engaging all of your senses to create a powerful, positive vision of the future you want. I used it extensively to imagine my immune system working to heal my body, shrinking my tumours, and restoring my health.

Dr. David Hamilton has some beautiful visualisations on his website that I practised daily. The incredible thing is that, on a physiological and emotional level, our minds respond to vivid imagination in much the same way as they do to reality. This means we can harness visualisation to activate neurological pathways that support healing, guiding our bodies toward wellness.

I even turned everyday moments into healing visualisations. Before my first operation, we took a short holiday, and I swam every day. As I moved through the water, I imagined it as a healing force, cleansing and restoring me with every stroke. Reframing experiences like this helped me feel empowered and gave my mind and body a sense of purpose in my recovery.

Before my operations, I had to use an antibacterial body wash as part of the preparation. Instead of seeing it as just another medical requirement, I chose to visualise it as a healing wash, supporting my recovery and protecting my body.

This is where the power of beliefs comes in - it doesn't have to be objectively true; it just needs to be useful, supportive, and kind to yourself. I chose to believe that the wash was keeping me safe and well, rather than seeing it as a reminder that my operation was getting closer. That simple shift in perspective made all the difference in how I felt about the process.

In the lead-up to my surgery, I focused on managing my emotions, making sure I stayed as positive as possible. Of course, there were moments when intrusive thoughts crept in, or I felt sad - and that was okay. I allowed myself to sit with those feelings for a while, but then I reminded myself that I had a choice. I could shift my focus using gratitude or a resource anchor to help me move through it (see Chapter 17).

Being kind and gentle with yourself during this time is so important. Whatever you are feeling is completely valid. I knew I would feel better - mentally and physically - if I chose to focus on something more positive, so that's what I did. It's all about choice.

One of the core principles I aim to live by is asking myself: 'Am I living at cause, or am I living at effect?' In essence, am I taking responsibility for my life, or am I placing blame elsewhere? This simple yet profound idea has been a game changer for me. It's not always easy but when I consciously choose to take accountability for my thoughts, actions, and responses, I feel more empowered and in control.

It's easy to fall into the trap of blaming others or even cancer for the situation we find ourselves in. However, when we do this, we give away our power. When we blame others or feel like we have no control over what's happening, it leaves us feeling disempowered. And when we feel powerless, it can be hard to take any meaningful action. None of us asked for cancer; however, blaming the disease or the situation and feeling like we're helpless is far from helpful. Instead, finding a way to reclaim our power and focus on what we can control can make all the difference.

For whatever reason, cancer was inside me. Yes, it was affecting me physically and attacking my healthy cells but that didn't mean it had to affect my emotions, thoughts, or beliefs. Those were still mine to control. My thoughts and beliefs gave me a sense of control in the situation - I could choose what I thought and believed. Cancer wasn't in the driver's seat of my mind; I was. This mindset empowered me to choose how I wanted to respond. Remember, the equation: Event + Response = Outcome. Having the ability to choose my response was incredibly empowering and truly helpful in navigating this journey.

I also chose not to see cancer as the enemy, but rather as a situation from which I wanted to learn. Believe me, it wasn't something I would have chosen but it became an opportunity, nonetheless. I understand that this perspective may feel like a stretch at times, but I found it to be incredibly helpful. Realising that cancer didn't have to determine my thoughts, dominate my emotions, or dictate my behaviours was truly empowering. It gave me a sense of control and a chance to shape how I responded, rather than letting it control me.

So, there I was, pre-surgery. I had spent the weeks leading up to it visualising healing, being kind to myself, and creating a resource anchor to help me stay flexible and resilient, no matter what the day might bring. I also made sure I was prepared practically, not just emotionally. I had my overnight bag packed, just in case, and painkillers ready if I needed them. My husband was all set to take me to the hospital and bring me home. Checking out what I'd need post-surgery and knowing what to expect helped me feel more prepared.

I also made sure that any work or other commitments were covered. It's important to give yourself the time and space to recover, so being prepared in advance allows you to focus your energy on healing rather than worrying about other things.

Before the operation, do everything you can to be in the best physical and mental state. One of the most important things is to make sure you are getting enough sleep. Aiming for the recommended 8 hours per night leading up to the surgery is so important. If sleep is a bit elusive, simple tools like focused breathing can help calm your system and prepare you for rest. To practise focused breathing, take a slow, gentle, and full breath in for a count of 4, then exhale for a count of 6. This activates the parasympathetic nervous system, helping reduce stress and anxiety, while also guiding you toward a restful night's sleep.

For more information on sleep, visit:
www.achieveyourgreatness.co.uk/the-secret-of-sleep.

Remember, you can always use your resource anchor whenever you need it, especially if the preparation process starts to feel overwhelming. Take things one step at a time and be kind to yourself as you move through it.

Now, when it comes to telling people what's happening, that's another important consideration which I will be covering in the next chapter.

#21 Tip

Unexpected emotions or memories may surface during this time - and that's completely natural.

See it as an opportunity to reflect, heal, and create space for moving forward.

Be kind to yourself and seek support if you need it.

#22 Tip

You can turn anything you do into a powerful visualisation for healing - whatever feels right for you.

Get creative! Imagine every sip of water nourishing and healing your body, every deep breath filling you with strength, or every step you take guiding you towards wellness.

The more you engage your mind in these positive images, the more you support your body's natural ability to heal.

#23 Tip

When you 'live at cause', you're taking responsibility for yourself - your thoughts, your actions, your mindset.

When you're 'living at effect', you're giving away your power by blaming things outside of you.

Shifting back to 'living at cause' puts you back in the driver's seat of your life.

#24 Tip

Preparation is key - both practically and emotionally.

CHAPTER 7 - TELLING PEOPLE

One of the other things you might choose to do as you approach your surgery is to share the news with others. This experience is very personal, and it's important to remember that it's unique to you. You know what feels right for you, so do what you feel comfortable with - there's no right or wrong way to handle it.

Before I had my full diagnosis and it was just 'likely' I had cancer, I only told a couple of people - my husband and my Mum. I'm an auditory processor, which means I work through things by talking. It's how I process and do my best thinking! You might find that you have a different way of processing - perhaps you prefer to write things down, reflect quietly on your own, or use another method. It's all about personal preference.

After my diagnosis, I did eventually tell those closest to me - those I knew would support me in a positive and uplifting way. However, I quickly realised that after a while, I didn't want to talk about it anymore. I had processed what I needed to, and discussing it wasn't helping - it was just firing off the neurological pathways that weren't serving me well. When we went on holiday, we spoke about it only a few times, and I consciously made space for a week of normality.

Ask yourself, 'What do I need right now?' Do you feel the need to talk it through? Is it helping you? If so, that's great. If not, that's perfectly okay too. I didn't go public with my situation until after the operation because I needed time to process, heal, and prepare myself - physically and mentally - and even then, it was only with close friends and family.

I did, however, share the news with a few of my clients and publicly mentioned that I'd be taking a month off without specifying the reason. You know your own circumstances better than anyone else - what will work for you? And it's completely okay to change your mind as things unfold.

From my experience with previous operations, I knew I'd need a quiet time to heal after the surgery. I let a few close friends and family members know this in advance. While we kept in touch via messages, I didn't want visitors during that time. I knew I needed to conserve my energy and focus solely on healing. And again, that's perfectly fine. You know what you need, and it's important to honour that. Feel confident to ask for help too - whether it's emotional support or practical assistance. It's okay to ask for what you need.

It's easy to fall into the trap of expecting others to 'mindread' - thinking they should automatically know how we're feeling or what we need. And if their actions don't match our expectations, we can feel hurt or misunderstood. For example, if people message you rather than phone, you could mindread that they didn't care or had forgotten you … alternatively, maybe they don't want to disturb you if you are resting.

It's a good reminder that everyone sees things differently and being open and clear about what we need can help avoid misunderstandings. If we are unable to find out what another person is thinking, then I suggest that you make up something positive and helpful rather than mindreading something negative.

If you want to talk to someone, reach out - give them a call or let them know you'd appreciate a chat or help. This was a tough lesson for me since I'm naturally very independent. I had to ask my husband to help me with things I'd never imagined, like pulling off my surgical support stockings so I could shower and then putting them back on. It was a new experience for both of us! It taught me how important it is to ask for what you need and allow others to support you.

As mentioned previously, one of the important lessons I learnt was to give myself time to process the information before sharing it with others. After the wait I mentioned earlier, the day finally came to discover the results of the operation. I had expected to know the outcome one way or another, but I wasn't prepared for a mixed result ... part of the operation had been successful, and the other part was unclear. This led to another four weeks of waiting. I needed time to process this uncertainty - to talk it through with my husband and Mum, to wrap my head around it, and to prepare for how others might react.

I'm incredibly grateful for the amazing support system I have around me - people I can talk to, be real with, and share the good and less good times together. I encourage you to build your own support system too, as the reactions you get when sharing mixed news can be quite interesting.

There can be extreme reactions, and often, both ends of the spectrum can be less than helpful. If you've ever heard Brené Brown talk about the difference between empathy and sympathy, you will know exactly what I mean. She explains that empathy never starts with the phrase 'at least ...' For example, 'At least they got one cancer out!' While that may be true and is certainly one way of looking at it, I wasn't ready to hear that right away. I needed time to process and find gratitude for that perspective on my own - perhaps overnight, not immediately.

Remember, people are only trying to help. Many simply don't know what to say or how to react. I recall when my dad had cancer, one of his friends stopped visiting because they didn't know how to approach him.

Instead of taking this personally, I realised that they were doing the best they could, likely struggling themselves with how to come to terms with what was happening - or just unsure of what to say.

People *are* doing the best they can with the resources they have available - and we all have moments when we feel less than resourceful. A little patience and understanding can make all the difference with ourselves as well as others.

#25 Tip

It is your choice whether you tell people or not.

Ask for what you need and surround yourself with those who can support you - whether that means being there to listen or respecting your need for space.

#26 Tip

Don't expect others to read your mind.

If you need something, ask.

It not only helps you get the support you need but also gives others the chance to support you and contribute.

#27 Tip

Give yourself time to process before sharing your news.

If you know the person you are going to tell may respond negatively or with toxic positivity*, make sure you are emotionally prepared beforehand.

Let their response roll off you like water off a duck's back!

*Toxic positivity is where there is a positive spin on everything without empathy. It is good to be positive - in a gentle way, at the right time and only when appropriate for the other person.

CHAPTER 8 - COMPARING YOURSELF TO OTHERS

This is an interesting topic because it's so easy to do - comparing our situation to someone else's. Many of us do this naturally and it can be unhelpful. It can create unnecessary pressure. If two people had the same surgery, and one is up and about within hours, but the other is struggling, they may feel down, as if they are not measuring up, or that things are unfair. Remember, everyone is different.

If you happen to be doing better than someone else, be mindful of not letting your ego take over. It's important to keep perspective and be grateful for your progress. Your journey is unique to you, and comparing yourself to others doesn't always serve you.

There are times when hearing from others about their experiences can be helpful, especially when it reduces feelings of isolation and helps you feel more prepared. For instance, after my surgery, I was bright blue all over - I looked like a Smurf! Seeing someone else on the ward who was slightly blue reassured me that it was normal (due to the dye used for the sentinel lymph node biopsy). Remember, you don't have to be like everyone else. If you are not sure about something, ask.

There are times when comparison can actually be helpful, especially if you are feeling sorry for yourself. It can help put things into perspective. After my diagnosis, everything seemed to revolve around cancer, especially as I was waiting for results and the next steps. Sometimes, comparison came my way (rather than me actively seeking it), and I found it helpful.

One evening before my first operation, we watched a movie about a baseball player. I hadn't read the synopsis beforehand, and it turned out the main character had bone cancer and passed away within 18 months. Probably not the best movie to watch the night before surgery but I chose (and remember, we always have a choice) to reframe the situation. I reminded myself how fortunate I was that my cancer had been caught early, that medical science had advanced so much since then, and that I was in a very different situation. It helped me put things into perspective and stopped me from feeling sorry for myself.

That experience reminded me that even when comparisons arise, we can choose how to interpret them - and sometimes, they can shift our perspective in a helpful way.

#28 Tip

Remember, your journey is unique.

Comparing yourself to others can be unhelpful and may create unnecessary pressure.

Focus on your own path and progress.

#29 Tip

If comparison helps you gain a healthier perspective, then great - just make sure it isn't coming from a place of ego or victimhood, such as thinking you are 'better' or 'worse off' than someone else.

At the end of the day, we are all human.

None of us asked for this journey, and some may face a tougher road than others.

We are not better or worse than anyone else; we are simply different and unique.

CHAPTER 9 - THE DAY OF THE SURGERY

The day eventually arrived. I made sure I was as prepared as I could be. I used my resource anchor throughout - especially when I found out that my tumours hadn't disappeared as I had hoped, and surgery was still necessary. I was the last patient to go down that day, so it was a long wait. I spent my time reading, chatting with other patients and nurses, and using gratitude in my quiet moments. I focused on my breathing to manage stress and keep myself in the best possible state for the surgery.

The flexibility anchor was incredibly important, and I made sure to find things that would make me laugh during the day - those light moments were essential. Managing my emotional state that day was critical for my mental well-being. I took the time to chat with others on the ward and offer support in whatever way I could. Sometimes, when things are tough for you, helping others is the best way to feel better. I even offered to assist the nursing staff, who seemed a bit overwhelmed; however, funnily enough, they didn't take me up on the offer!

I used the same process for all three of my operations - making sure I had all the resources I needed ahead of time.

Historically, operations had been a source of fear for me. Several years ago, my father was given too much anaesthetic during surgery, which led to a heart attack. This experience created a deep-seated fear and belief that I would die on the operating table. However, I had done some work to change that belief and remove my fear, allowing me to approach my surgery with a sense of calm.

There was a time, before I discovered NLP and had learnt how to change my beliefs, when I had an operation and was sent home because my blood pressure was too high for the surgery to go ahead. My emotions had taken a toll on my physical state, which demonstrates just how much our thoughts can affect our well-being.

This time, however, my blood pressure was normal due to the resource anchor, and I was home just a couple of hours after the surgery.

See Chapter 17 for tools to help change beliefs and remove unwanted emotions.

And then, my focus shifted to recovery.

#30 Tip

Finding ways to help others can shift your focus and bring positivity, even in tough situations.

Similarly, finding things that make you laugh and practising gratitude can uplift your spirits during challenging times.

#31 Tip

Ensure you are emotionally prepared for your operation ahead of time.

Take the necessary steps to create resources for yourself, as outlined in Chapter 17.

This will help you approach the day with a sense of calm and readiness.

CHAPTER 10 - POST-SURGERY

One of the key factors in recovery is sleep. As I've mentioned before, it's crucial before surgery and it's just as important for your healing afterwards. Being present and focusing on your breathing can help calm your mind, making it easier to fall asleep and allowing your body to rest and recover.

Keeping pain under control is also important during recovery. I believe that NLP can complement medical advice. I followed the recommended painkiller schedule but one night, I found myself unable to sleep due to the pain, despite having taken the prescribed amount.

To deal with this, I used a technique to minimise the pain. You can focus on a specific area of your body and direct energy there to change how it feels. For example, close your eyes and imagine you are holding a lemon. Picture cutting it into quarters and bringing one to your mouth. Notice how you may start to salivate; your body responds to the mere thought of eating a lemon. You can apply the same process to create a soothing, healing sensation, then imagine directing that feeling to the area of pain, helping to ease it.

I'm sure you've experienced a headache at some point and noticed how it tends to dominate your thoughts - it's all you can think about. However, if you start watching something engaging on TV or have a conversation with someone, you might find that the pain becomes less noticeable.

In the same way, if you shift your focus - perhaps by wiggling your toes or gently stroking your hands or face - it can help distract your mind from the pain. Shifting your attention to something neutral or soothing can lessen the intensity of discomfort.

For the first three weeks after the operation, I found myself waking up in the middle of the night, feeling restless and needing to walk. The surgical stockings felt hot and restrictive, so I would walk around the room focusing on what I was grateful for and gently stroked my hands and face, using a technique from the Havening Technique.

After a short while, I felt so much better and was able to return to sleep, feeling more at ease.

By listening to what my body needed, I was able to soothe it in a way that worked best for me. What does your body need?

There's research that shows laughter can be a great healer. For a while, I made sure to watch comedies that made me laugh out loud (thank you, *Miranda*!). This was particularly helpful in the first week after surgery when I wasn't as mobile. Laughter helped shift my mood and lighten the emotional load by releasing endorphins - the feel-good hormones. I used humour a lot during my recovery. It was my way of creating some distance from the situation, gaining a lighter perspective, and not taking everything so seriously.

There are also less helpful ways to manage pain. Things like overeating or drinking might provide temporary relief, but they can have a negative impact on your overall health. Whenever possible, it's a good idea to choose healthier methods. Meditation, visualisation, watching comedies, or reading uplifting books are all great alternatives that can help support your healing journey and keep your mind in a positive space.

During my recovery, I spent a lot of time meditating. There are many different types of meditation, ranging from guided sessions to simply sitting in silence. Meditation is a powerful way to align and calm your nervous system, supporting your recovery.

One of my favourite practices is chakra meditation, which you can easily find on YouTube. I also enjoyed healing sound baths, which you can listen to while lying at home recovering.

Another practice I found deeply soothing was the full-body scan meditation. In this practice, I would slow my breathing - inhaling gently and fully for a count of four, and exhaling to release any tension, unwanted emotions, or simply to let go. I would start at my toes, noticing and wiggling them, feeling gratitude for them. I'd then move slowly up my body, giving attention to each part - my feet, my legs, and so on.

One day, as I focused on my body, I was reminded of how I had once broken my toes, and how wonderfully my body had healed them. I felt deep gratitude for that healing process. As I continued, I reflected on other areas of my body that had healed over time, such as an upset stomach, and how naturally my body restored itself.

When I reached the area of my surgery, I sent healing energy there, just as I had for the other parts of my body. I felt an overwhelming sense of gratitude for the incredible healing power of my body, knowing that it was working tirelessly to heal this area as well. It was a truly amazing experience, and the sense of peace and gratitude it brought me was invaluable.

You will likely be given some exercises to do - and like me, they might not be easy at first. However, I started to see each one as a step on my journey to recovery. With every set, I felt like I was getting closer to being my fully fit self again. It really helped to reframe my mindset.

As part of my preparation, I made sure to have plenty of things lined up to enjoy during my recovery - a stack of books, great movies, and plenty of audios to listen to. These were an absolute lifesaver! Make sure you have some wonderful things ready for yourself too. For me, it felt like a blissful retreat - no need to worry about vacuuming or ironing (I was told I couldn't do those ... and I think they said *forever*?!). So, I took the opportunity to relax and do all the things I never have time for. It really was a silver lining in what wasn't an easy situation.

If you are anything like me, always busy with life, having this time to reconnect with myself, meditate, learn, recover, and heal was such a blessing. It gave me space to start thinking about my future and what it might look like after cancer.

#32 Tip

Listen to your body and give it what it needs.

Whether it's rest, movement, or distraction, honour what your body is telling you for a smoother recovery.

#33 Tip

Visualise a healing, soothing light radiating towards the area where you feel pain.

Focus on this light as it gently eases the discomfort and brings a sense of calm and healing to that part of your body.

Notice how the sensation shifts as you allow this healing energy to flow and soothe you.

#34 Tip

Make your recovery time as enjoyable as possible.

Surround yourself with things that make your heart sing
- whether that's listening to your favourite music,
watching movies, or diving into a good book.

If you can, spend some time in nature.

Nature has such amazing healing powers, and even if it's
just sitting by an open window and enjoying the view, it
can do wonders for your mental health.

CHAPTER 11 - FUTURE TREATMENTS

The thing about cancer is that it brings uncertainty and can stretch on for a while.

Even after surgeries, there are often additional treatments like radiotherapy, hormone therapy, immunotherapy or chemotherapy to go through.

Just like I visualised swimming as a healing power, as mentioned before, you can reframe the treatments you are receiving in a positive light. For instance, when I was going through radiotherapy, I imagined the rays as gentle, warming, and healing. I see the tablets I'm taking as something that's gentle and nurturing, with each one helping to support my recovery.

Also, remember to use the resource anchors you've created - and feel free to add to them or create new ones if you need extra support. They are there to help you throughout your journey and treatment.

Visualisation and meditation can be incredibly helpful, especially if your treatment takes time.

Taking the time to nurture your soul in this way will do wonders for your mental well-being.

#35 Tip

Remember, your beliefs are powerful and become your truth.

By visualising and reframing your treatments as healing, gentle, and soothing, you can support your recovery in a positive way.

#36 Tip

All the tools I've shared with you so far can be just as helpful during your treatments as they were before or after operations.

Keep using them - they are there to support you every step of the way.

CHAPTER 12 - YOUR FUTURE

During your recovery, once the first couple of weeks have passed and you hopefully start to feel a little better, it's a great time to think about your future. I went through several stages myself - the first being just surviving after the operation, taking it day by day until I began to feel more like myself. Be sure to be kind to yourself as you move through this phase - it might take some time, and that's okay.

Over the weeks that followed, as I slowly returned to a normal routine, I decided that I would prefer to focus on thriving - on how to move into the next phase of my life with more joy, gratitude, and love. Cancer was a wake-up call, and I want to make sure that the next 50 years of my life (or however long I have) are truly amazing.

What do you want your life to look like? None of us know what the future holds - sometimes, curveballs like cancer come our way. However, if we truly understand who we are at our core, beyond the labels we or others might place on us, we can navigate these challenging times with greater ease. Remember, you are so much more than just your diagnosis.

Understanding your purpose in life - what you are here to do, what brings you joy, and what helps others - is truly an amazing thing to discover. There's so much written about the purpose of life, with some people referring to it as their 'why' for living. What's your 'why'? Is it your family, friends, your work, or something else? Remember, there is only one of you - and that's you! An incredible, amazing, and fabulous person.

Being the best version of yourself is a beautiful purpose in life. Thinking about how you can be the best version and doing something, whether big or small, to help others can be incredibly rewarding. It can also bring light to the darker times. Whether it's being a wonderful parent, a supportive friend, showing kindness to a neighbour, caring for animals, volunteering, or simply sharing a smile - these acts can help you move forward into your future with purpose and positivity.

As Victor Frankl said in *Man's Search for Meaning*:

> 'It did not really matter what we expected from life, but rather what life expected from us. We needed to stop asking about the meaning of life, and instead to think of ourselves as those who were being questioned by life - daily and hourly.'

This idea completely changed my perspective. It moved me from questioning what it was all about to asking myself, 'What do I have to offer the world now and in the future?'

During cancer treatment, it can feel like your world revolves around your health, appointments, hospitals, uncertainty, and waiting. It's all about you for a while. Finding a way to focus on giving back, helping others, and contributing in some way can be such a beautiful transition back to normal life. It's a way to move forward, with purpose, after all you have been through.

For most of us, life will be different moving forward. Some may move on and be able to leave it behind, while others may face additional treatments and the ongoing emotional journey. Either way, we have a choice in how we want the rest of our lives to unfold. The past doesn't have to dictate your future. You can be whoever you want to be.

When we understand that we are all connected and that there is a higher purpose for our lives - that we're here for a reason - it can inspire us to take the time to truly discover who we are. This process can be incredibly positive and helpful as we think about the future and what it holds.

As I say, it doesn't have to be something huge. You don't need to solve global warming (though that would be pretty amazing if you could!). However, simple things, like visiting your neighbour, chatting with a friend who needs support, or even smiling at a stranger, can help you move forward into your new chapter. Truly feeling gratitude for everything you have - especially your health - is a powerful path to happiness.

Once you've reflected on your purpose - your 'why' for recovering and living - and spent time peeling away those labels of cancer to discover who you really are, you will start to recognise the qualities and characteristics that make you uniquely you. These are the things that transcend any situation and apply to every area of your life.

At this point, you can focus on ensuring your beliefs support you. Beliefs like 'I will survive,' 'I will get through this,' and 'I will be able to help others' were powerful affirmations that helped me push through even the toughest times.

This strong sense of self will help you navigate not just this challenge, but other hurdles life may throw your way. Realising that we have the power to be the architects of our lives, no matter the circumstances, is both liberating and exciting. It puts us back in the driver's seat of our own journey. I made the decision that cancer wouldn't define me. As Abraham Lincoln said, 'Most folks are about as happy as they make up their minds to be.'

Once the initial shock and adjustment phases have passed, it's a great time to start reflecting on all of this. Take your time, and when you are ready, you can begin to embrace happiness in the way that feels right for you, by applying what you are learning along the way.

Many people, me included, like to set goals or outcomes for the future, which is great. Throughout this process, my main outcome was to be completely healthy. Every step I took, I asked myself: 'Is this aligned with my goal of being well?'

In NLP, we talk about 'well-formed outcomes' - setting ourselves up for success by clearly defining what we want. This means visualising what the outcome looks and feels like, knowing how we will recognise when we've achieved it, and ensuring it's positively stated.

For example, rather than saying 'I don't want to have cancer', a more powerful statement is 'I want to be totally healthy'. This is because our brains don't process negation well - if we say 'cancer-free', the brain first registers 'cancer' before processing 'free from it'. By focusing on 'feeling healthy, being healthy', we reinforce the outcome we actually want.

If 'being completely healthy' feels like too big a goal, break it down into smaller, achievable steps, for example:

- Walking around the park on your own.

- Climbing the stairs easily.

- Sleeping comfortably through the night.

Setting smaller milestones, with target dates, helps focus the mind and supports recovery.

It's also important to consider the ecology of your outcomes - this means thinking about what you will gain or lose by achieving them. Taking the time to ensure our goals align with all areas of our life can make all the difference.

Another important aspect of planning for the future is considering the experiences you want to have - both now and later (as mentioned previously). However, what if you are not physically well enough to do them yet?

That's what I faced. My '50 things for 50' list included indoor skydiving, paddleboarding, and learning to dance - none of which I could do immediately. I had two choices: postpone them (which I did for some) or not do them at all ... however, using NLP there is another way.

Every activity we pursue serves a purpose - it fulfils a need or has a positive intention. We seek instant gratification in different ways: we eat to feel satisfied, laugh for joy, or hug loved ones to feel connection. By understanding the deeper purpose behind our desired experiences, we can find alternative ways to fulfil those needs while we recover.

Most of us believe we need to *do* something in order to *feel* a certain way. This is a natural cause-and-effect reaction - whether positive or negative. For example, we see something funny and laugh, which makes us feel good. Conversely, if we see something sad and cry, it makes us feel down.

However, when we learn to manage our emotions (as discussed earlier), we realise that we don't always need an external trigger - we can create an *internal* one instead.

Our minds are incredibly powerful. History has shown time and again that people who visualise their desired outcomes often achieve them.

By visualising an activity we want to do, or by asking ourselves what deeper emotional need that activity fulfils, we gain a better understanding of our true motivations. This allows us to tap into the feelings we seek, even before we physically experience them.

For example, if skydiving gives you a sense of excitement and adventure, take a moment to visualise the experience. Imagine, in your mind's eye, what it would feel like; what you would see, hear, and say to yourself. Once you are fully immersed in that imagined experience, ask yourself: 'What is this really giving me at a deeper level?'

Beyond the thrill of the jump, you might realise it provides a sense of freedom, joy, adventure, or lightness. Allow yourself to fully experience these emotions through your visualisation. Then, take it a step further, ask yourself: 'What's even deeper or more important than this?'

You may find that the answer is something profound - perhaps love, connection, oneness, or a deep sense of inner peace. Often, these deeper feelings transcend any specific activity and instead connect us to a greater sense of self or bliss.

You can repeat this process as many times as you like until you reach a state that is independent of circumstances, people, or activities - one that feels pure and deeply fulfilling. Allow yourself to fully embrace this feeling and take a mental note of it. You might even associate it with a colour or a word so that whenever you see that colour or say that word, it instantly brings you back to that emotional state.

#37 Tip

Remember, you are amazing, and your future - however long it may be - is yours to create; the choice is in your hands.

#38 Tip

Set well-formed goals for your future, whether small - like going for a walk - or larger, such as achieving full recovery and health.

Clear, positive goals help focus your mind and support your recovery.

#39 Tip

If you are unable to do the activities you desire, visualise
experiencing them and explore the deeper need
they fulfil.

These powerful states such as love, peace, bliss, aren't
limited to specific activities; you can access them
anytime, anywhere.

CHAPTER 13 - MORE CURVEBALLS!

If your experience is anything like mine, you may face more curveballs than you ever expected! My first diagnosis was a huge setback; however, it wasn't the only one. Life often brings not just one challenge, but many. How these setbacks affect us depends on how we choose to see them.

I received the results from my first operation, and they weren't as I had hoped - it was only partially successful due to an error, meaning I needed another operation. This was a difficult reality to accept. It took me a full day to process this news and mentally prepare for the next steps. Emotionally, I didn't get angry because I knew that would be a waste of energy - energy I needed for healing.

Resilience

Resilience, a word you've likely heard, became crucial for me. It can be defined as 'the ability to bounce back from setbacks and the mental and emotional strength to navigate life's challenges and thrive.'

Some of the tools I used during this time were the resource anchor and focusing on reframing the situation, reminding myself that everything happens for a reason. I also held onto the idea of choice - I chose to delay the operation for a couple of months. Medically, it wasn't going to make much difference, and I had a list of things I wanted to do and enjoy before the next surgery. Running my own company added another layer of complexity - if I don't work, I don't earn money!

One of the keys to resilience, I believe, is recognising that what you are going through is finite - that there is an end in sight. It may be a little way off but there will be an end. This mindset gave me significant power. I love the idea of taking an astronaut's view on life - floating above the world and looking down.

We can apply this by visualising ourselves floating above our life, seeing our path laid out below us, with the past in one direction and the future in another. From this elevated 'bird's-eye' view, we can gain a different perspective on what's happening. Knowing that what I was going through was just a point in time - there was a before and there would be an after - helped me realise that it wasn't forever. In the grand scheme of life, what was happening was just a short moment.

If the 'after' feels less than easy to picture, break it down into smaller steps. For example, rather than focusing on finishing all your treatment, focus on completing just your next session.

As I've mentioned before, none of us really know how long we have on this earth - some of us may have a clearer idea than others. One of the great resources I found during this time was Eckhart Tolle's book *The Power of Now*. It's an incredible read that teaches us to truly make the most of each moment. After all, we only have the present. Yesterday is behind us, and none of us can predict what tomorrow will bring. By focusing on the now, I was able to stay grounded, centred, and positive, which made a huge difference in how I faced the challenges ahead.

At times, it can feel all-consuming. However, when you look at life from this elevated perspective, you can start to notice all the other blessings you have; friends, family, a roof over your head, air to breathe and everything we've previously mentioned when practising gratitude. All the experiences you've had and will have again serve as reminders that you will get through this. This view also helped me realise the importance of making the most of every minute, appreciating the small moments along the way.

During the waiting period before my next operation, I chose to focus on creating positive experiences. I launched a book and had an amazing launch event with some of my favourite people by my side. I spent time with friends and family, enjoyed coffees and lunches with loved ones, took walks on the beach, and attended Christmas events. All these moments helped to top up my emotional reserves, giving me beautiful memories to draw upon during my recovery and the more challenging times.

I believe it was Einstein who once said, 'The definition of insanity is doing the same thing over and over again and expecting different results.' This really resonated with me. I certainly didn't want to repeat the same experience; however, the reality was that I had very little control over what was happening. I was in the hands of the medical team, and there was no way I could physically influence what would take place on the operating table while I was unconscious.

What I *could* control, though, was my mindset - how I managed my emotions and responses. As I've mentioned before, emotional resilience played a huge role in my recovery. Although I couldn't control the physical aspects of the surgery, I could choose how I reacted to the situation, and that made all the difference in maintaining a sense of calm and empowerment throughout the process.

I took some time to really think about what I could do differently this time, to ensure that the outcome of the operation would be a success. I wanted to understand what went wrong before and how I could do everything possible to make sure things went smoothly this time around.

One technique I used was called the New Behaviour Generator (see Chapter 17). The procedure required the radiologist to insert guiding wires before the operation, which had been placed incorrectly last time. So, I used this technique to visualise how I would manage my state during the wire insertion. I practised staying calm, and mentally rehearsed checking with the specialist to ensure the wire was inserted correctly.

By practising over and over, I was essentially creating new neurological pathways - like a dress rehearsal. This way, when I was in the actual situation, I knew exactly how I would behave and feel. The more I visualised this, the more confident I became that I could handle the situation calmly and effectively.

While I couldn't control the outcome of the operation itself, I made sure I did everything within my power to help ensure it went well. For example, when the first guiding wire was inserted, I asked for it to be checked, and sure enough, it had moved out of place. They had to redo it, and it took them a while to get it positioned in the right place.

During that time, I remained patient and calm, using my anchors to stay resourceful and grounded while they worked on me before the operation. I knew I had done everything I could to set things up for success. At that point, the only thing left was to let go and trust that everything would unfold as it needed.

There was another 5-week wait for the results of this operation, and they weren't entirely sure if the operation was successful. It was another curveball. Naturally, doubt crept in. What if it hadn't been successful?

I knew that going down a path of worry wouldn't help but I didn't want to ignore those thoughts either. So, I gave myself a moment to think things through. I allowed myself to consider what I would do if it wasn't successful. After a brief period of planning and considering my options, I decided that if needed, I would opt for a mastectomy, since the cancer was difficult to reach.

Once I had my plan B in place, I consciously decided to stop dwelling on it. I shifted my focus back to healing and trusting that the procedure had been successful. And, of course, I watched Christmas movies! It felt like I had organised my backup plan, tucked it away on the shelf, and was free to move forward with positivity and belief in my recovery.

My recovery from the second operation was incredibly different from the first - it was so much quicker! I was almost back to normal within just a couple of days. It was amazing. The lesson I took from this experience is that life often unfolds differently than we expect - sometimes better, sometimes less so. If we know we have the inner resources to handle whatever comes our way and the flexibility to move through challenges with grace, then those curveballs become less daunting. We can cope with them and, in time, get back to living our lives more quickly.

The day finally arrived for the results of my second operation and there was more uncertainty. Once again, they were not sure whether the second operation had been successful. I had to wait to find out if everything had gone to plan. This time, it was only a two-week wait until the next tests and consultations. However, during that time, I noticed an unhelpful belief starting to creep in.

Because the situation seemed to mirror what had happened after my first operation, my mind began to think that the same thing would happen again - that I would need a third operation. This is a natural response from our brains. When we go through an event, our unconscious mind tries to make sense of it by searching for similar past experiences. In my case, the situation was eerily similar to what I'd experienced just a couple of months earlier.

This is where the brain's natural filtering process kicks in. We have what is called a 'generalisation filter', which helps us quickly make sense of the world. It's why we can recognise things like chairs without needing to relearn what a chair looks like every time we see one! Our brain categorises experiences into neat little boxes, which helps us move through life more efficiently. While this is incredibly useful for things like chairs, it can be less helpful when it causes us to generalise a past event - such as a surgery not going to plan - and assume that the next surgery will be the same.

Recognising this pattern was key for me. I had to remind myself that just because one surgery didn't go as expected doesn't mean the next one would be the same. Each situation is unique, and it was important for me to separate the two.

Being self-aware is so important because it allows you to spot unhelpful patterns like this as they arise. The more you learn about yourself, the more self-aware you become. I realised that I needed to challenge and change this belief that I'd need yet another operation. To do this, I used a powerful tool called Core Transformation created by Connirae Andreas. This process allowed me to work with the part of me that was holding onto the belief, helping me shift it.

The core states I achieved through this work were peace and wholeness - states that I held onto for the next two weeks as I awaited the results. It was incredibly helpful in keeping me grounded and centred during this uncertain time. If you are curious about Core Transformation, you can learn more by reading Connirae Andreas' book, *Core Transformation*, or by attending a course at www.achieveyourgreatness.co.uk. You can also use the belief change tool which you can find in Chapter 17.

I knew I needed patience and resilience during this time. I also focused on cultivating peace, so that the next couple of weeks would be positive, and uplifting, rather than filled with worry, anxiety, and stress. It wasn't easy; however, I knew I had a choice in how I responded.

By shifting my focus to everything I was grateful for, I was able to keep my mindset positive. I also started Deepak Chopra's '21-Days of Abundance' meditation (which is available on YouTube). It's an amazing, uplifting meditation that helps you focus on abundance, especially in terms of health. It's a gentle yet powerful tool to help you stay grounded and optimistic.

#40 Tip

Life isn't perfect, and setbacks are a part of the journey.

If we expect perfection, we may be disappointed.

When we accept life's ups and downs and develop useful resources, we become more flexible and resilient - helping us get back on our feet faster.

#41 Tip

Taking a bird's eye view of your situation can help you
realise that what you are experiencing is just a point in
time - it will pass, and there will be an 'after' to
the challenge.

#42 Tip

Give yourself time to process and sit with less than easy decisions.

Use the New Behaviour Generator technique (see Chapter 17) to rehearse difficult conversations or situations.

This can help you feel calmer, know what you want to say, and be prepared for how you want to react when the actual event happens.

CHAPTER 14 - OVERTHINKING

I've always had what I call a 'busy brain!' If you are anything like me, you will know exactly what I mean - constantly thinking, coming up with new ideas, plans, and schemes. My mind is always buzzing with something.

Now, there's absolutely nothing wrong with thinking, but it is worth checking in with yourself to see if your thoughts are positive and helpful. If they are not, those are the ones you may want to change. There are many reasons why our thoughts can turn negative - limiting beliefs and past experiences can often play a big role. If you are finding that your thoughts are leaning in this direction and turning into negative beliefs, then look at Chapter 17 for strategies on how to shift these. It's important because negative thinking can have a mental and physical impact and making small adjustments can really make a difference.

After receiving the inconclusive results from my second operation, I found my mind going into overdrive. Speaking to others in similar situations, I realised I wasn't alone in this. The first night, I lay awake, my mind racing through everything - from Christmas plans to dinner, moving, holidays ... nothing that really related to the news I had just received. My thoughts were darting all over the place.

The next day I knew I had to do something to move past all the overthinking - after all, there's always something to think about! I needed to calm my mind - not only so I could sleep, which is essential for both health and healing, but also so I could find peace.

It's easy to think that our conscious mind, the part of us that does all the thinking, is who we really are. However, in reality, it's just a part of us. Sure, it's an important part, just like our heart, lungs, legs, or feet but it is only one aspect of who we are. We can control our feet, wiggling them or keeping them still. The same goes for our thoughts. With practice, we can learn to control our thoughts too. And, considering how powerful they are in shaping our reality, learning to control them is essential for creating the life we want.

One of the ways I started managing my overactive thinking was through meditation. At first, I could barely manage 10 seconds without my mind running off in all directions. I reminded myself that it was just a few minutes away from my thoughts, and I could always think again afterwards. So, I tried again - and I did a bit better.

I found that guided meditation was especially helpful, particularly in the beginning, because it gave me some structure, instead of just sitting in silence with my thoughts. As I mentioned earlier, I love Deepak Chopra's '21 Days of Abundance' meditation. Some mornings, I realised I'd drifted off and was back to thinking about everything again, so I'd simply repeat the day's session until I could stay present and keep my mind quiet for a little longer. It wasn't perfect at first but with consistency, I noticed it becoming easier over time.

I still had a way to go, yet I realised that beyond my busy thoughts, there was a place of peace - and that was where I needed to be. So, I made peace my focus, just like I would focus on work, exercise, or any other aspect of my life. Meditation and my health became priorities.

In NLP, we have a great principle that there is no such thing as failure, only feedback. So, when I found myself drifting into thought rather than meditating, I didn't beat myself up. I simply let it go, refocused my mind, and carried on. It became less about perfection and more about progress, which helped me stay calm and patient with myself along the way.

Every behaviour we have - whether it's overthinking, worrying, or anything else - has a positive intention behind it. It's often driven by an emotion and a need we're trying to fulfil. Once we understand this, we can see that if a behaviour isn't serving us in the long run, we have the power to change it.

In the case of overthinking, one night of it might be okay but I knew I needed sleep to heal, especially during such a challenging time. So, I decided to change this behaviour. For a helpful tool on how to do this, check out the 'New Behaviour Generator' in Chapter 17.

I recognised that, to get through the waiting periods, I needed to focus on how I wanted things to be. Shifting my mindset and creating a mental picture of a positive outcome was a powerful way to manage my thoughts and emotions during this time. When we focus on what we want rather than getting stuck in worry, we begin to take charge of our experience, helping us move through challenges with more ease.

Finally, the day came for my next set of mammograms; the cancer was still there and hadn't been removed in the second surgery. The surgeon and radiologist explained what had happened and outlined how the process would be different the next time. Unfortunately, I did need to have a third operation. As I had mentioned earlier, I had already made the decision that if things went wrong again, I would opt for a mastectomy. However, after discussing it with the team, they advised against it.

There was definitely a temptation for me to stick to my original decision of having a mastectomy. However, I knew at this point that it wasn't about my pride or stubbornness - it was about making the right decision for me.

It's okay to change your mind. Sometimes, as we gather more information, our perspective evolves. What felt like the right choice at one point may no longer seem the best option. Embrace the flexibility to adjust your decisions as needed.

Stress

When I heard that I might need a third operation, it triggered the stress response in my body. As mentioned previously, when we experience stress, the amygdala activates, putting us into fight, flight, or freeze mode. Historically, this response helped us react quickly to physical dangers. However, nowadays, even when we're not physically in danger, our bodies can still send out the same biochemical responses.

Being aware of this response allowed me to process the information, I could then apply techniques to reset my emotional state and feel more positive and grounded.

Understanding the science behind our reactions can help us regain control and move through challenges more effectively.

As Gabor Maté points out in his book, *When the Body Says No*, 'research literature has identified three factors that universally lead to stress: *uncertainty, lack of information, and loss of control*.'

In that moment, I realised all three of these factors were at play. However, here's the thing: I also knew that I had a choice. I could sit there and wallow in self-pity, questioning why this was happening again, blaming myself or others, and feeling like life was unfair - or I could take action and address those factors head-on.

After coming home from the hospital, I spent the next day trying to process all the information I'd been given. I went through every letter, piecing everything together in an effort to make sense of what had gone wrong. Along the way, I uncovered gaps and more questions that needed answering before I moved forward with the next operation. This time, I didn't want to wait - I wanted it done as quickly as possible.

Lack of information

The lack of information factor was the biggest issue for me. My logical brain had questions, and I knew I wouldn't feel at peace until I filled in the gaps in my knowledge. So, I wrote out my concerns and realised I needed a second opinion to ensure I was understanding the situation correctly. I also wanted to be able to explain my concerns clearly to the surgeon.

When we are emotional or stressed, our communication can be less effective. This is due to the stress response mentioned earlier, in which activity in the prefrontal cortex - the part of the brain responsible for rational, logical thinking - is reduced as the amygdala becomes overactive. The prefrontal cortex is also responsible for language processing, perspective taking and emotional regulation, which is why it can become less easy to communicate when stressed. I needed to make sure I expressed myself in the best way possible.

Therefore, I used my resource anchor to calm my mind, and I arranged to meet my brother to talk things through. If you have a need, it's important to figure out what that need is and then determine who's best equipped to help.

It may sound obvious; however, if you are dealing with a logical problem, it's helpful to talk to someone who is slightly detached from the situation and can provide a rational perspective - not someone directly involved. Likewise, if you are dealing with an emotional issue, make sure you talk to someone who can support you emotionally.

In my case, I needed logical reasoning, which is why I turned to my brother. He would be able to offer that, along with emotional support if needed. It's like getting a plumber to fix your hot water system, rather than an electrician - it just works better when you choose the right person!

Having that meeting set up with my brother really helped me feel more in control. I knew I would get the support I needed, and I would be able to ask questions in the right way to make sure I got my point across clearly when I spoke with the surgeon.

Loss of control

The 'loss of control' factor, which I've mentioned before, was still something I needed to explore further. However, I knew I still had choices - whether to go for a mastectomy or a third lumpectomy on that cancer. I also knew I had control over my response. I could get angry and upset, or I could choose a different, more constructive response.

While it wasn't easy, I reminded myself that I needed to focus on what I could control - my response. Getting angry at the person who would be performing the surgery wasn't going to be helpful, especially since he was the one holding the scalpel!

Uncertainty

The other element, 'uncertainty,' was interesting because it had started to subside for me. Yes, there was still uncertainty about whether the third operation would be successful, but I chose to focus on the things I could control to create a sense of certainty. I organised my work, moved courses around, and focused on the tasks and decisions that were within my power. By taking small, manageable steps to organise and plan, I found I could bring a sense of order to my life, which helped ease the uncertainty.

The decision I faced was definitely a tough one. With so much uncertainty about the outcome, a loss of faith in the system, and the thought of going under the knife once again, it wasn't easy. Gathering as much information as I could, as mentioned before, was crucial to making an informed decision that felt right for me.

What I didn't realise until a few years ago is that we actually have not just one brain, but three. We have clusters of neurons not only in our head, but also in our heart and gut. Science shows that both the heart and gut contain complex networks of neurons, sometimes called the 'heart brain' and 'gut brain', which influence how we think and feel. So, when it came to deciding, I knew it needed to feel right in all three areas. I believe that wisdom lies in aligning my gut (intuition), head (logic), and heart (emotion). When all three are in harmony, I feel confident I'm making the right choice.

As I've mentioned before, in NLP we often talk about having both a conscious mind - the logical, thinking part and an unconscious mind - the feeling, intuitive part, and the storehouse of our learned experiences. I needed to ensure that both were aligned and on board with the decision, which helped guide me toward what felt best for me.

I decided to call the hospital the next day to let them know I had some questions I'd like to discuss with the surgeon.

When I spoke to the surgeon, I was able to ask all the logical questions I had prepared, and he gave me the answers I needed. That conversation helped me feel much more at peace with my decision, which in turn reduced my stress response.

Of course, there were no guarantees. My surgeon did mention that I might need a mastectomy later; however, I knew that for this moment, the decision to go ahead with the lumpectomy was the right one for me. It may not be the right choice for everyone, but it felt right for me, and that's what mattered in that moment.

As mentioned, one of the key factors that can contribute to stress is a lack of information. One of the easiest ways to reduce stress in this area is to ask questions and gather knowledge. However, it's important to be cautious about who you ask - ensure that you are getting your answers from the right people, particularly those with professional expertise.

Another important area of knowledge to consider is how to manage our emotions and responses. Often, people feel stressed or stuck simply because they don't know how to move forward. I was certainly in this position myself before I learnt about NLP. I highly recommend that you apply the tools in this book or attend an NLP course to expand your understanding of how to manage your emotional responses. This way, instead of feeling like a victim or a passive bystander in your situation, you can take an active role in choosing your responses and how you feel. Knowledge empowers you to create more control and peace in your life.

It's important to remember that it's perfectly normal to feel the emotions you're experiencing. Suppressing or repressing them can lead to problems later, so it's crucial to acknowledge and express your feelings in a healthy way.

Friends of mine have a wonderful model called the ALE model, which can be really helpful in managing emotions. (*The Little Book of Resilience*, Joe and Melody Cheal).

- The first step is to **Acknowledge** the emotion you are feeling, whether it's anger, sadness, frustration, or something else.

- Then, **Label it** - simply identify what you are feeling, for example, 'I am feeling angry right now'.

- Finally, **Express it**. This could mean talking to someone you trust, writing about it, going for a walk, or even punching a punch bag - whatever helps you release the emotion in a healthy, constructive way.

If you still feel a residue of that emotion after expressing it, then check out Chapter 17 where I cover techniques to collapse any unwanted emotions that might still be lingering. Expressing emotions is a vital part of processing them and preventing them from building up over time.

The day of my third operation arrived, and I knew that this time, I needed to do even more to protect my mental health.

The woman next to me had just come out of a long operation, and the conversation was full of talk about risks, and complications - unsettling topics for me.

I immediately reached for my headphones and put on a meditation track to help me stay calm and focused. I also used my anchor to access my inner state of peace. This is the beauty of NLP - being self-aware allows you to recognise what you need in any given situation and, more importantly, gives you the tools to fulfil that need. In that moment, I had the power to choose my response, and I chose to protect my mental space with the techniques I had learnt.

In the book *When the Body Says No*, Gabor Maté talks about hidden stress and whether certain personality traits might make individuals more susceptible to illnesses like cancer. As I read, there were parts that really resonated with me. One of the most striking ideas was about putting others' needs before my own. It made me stop and reflect deeply on my own values and priorities - where did I fit into the equation?

You might be familiar with the concept of Johari's Window, which highlights the things others can see in us that we might not be aware of ourselves. *When the Body*

Says No served as an eye-opener in that sense. It gave me the chance to evaluate the patterns in my behaviour, the things I said and did, which often aligned with the personality traits Maté discussed.

This can be a crucial step in your journey - recognising and changing patterns of behaviour that no longer serve you. Take a moment to reflect on any habits or responses that might be holding you back. When you're ready, the 'New Behaviour Generator' technique in Chapter 17 can guide you in creating more helpful, empowering patterns.

#43 Tip

Beyond our thinking lies a place of peace - a calm,
centred space that we can access through meditation.

It's a space where we can quiet the constant chatter of
our minds and reconnect with a deeper sense
of tranquillity.

Meditation offers us the opportunity to step away from
our thoughts, to simply be present in the moment, and
to find stillness amidst the busyness of life.

It's in this peaceful space that we can begin to heal, gain
clarity, and cultivate a sense of balance.

The more we practise, the easier it becomes to access
that inner peace whenever we need it.

#44 Tip

The stress response is a natural reaction designed to protect us in times of extreme physical danger, helping us to either fight, flee, or freeze.

However, this response can be less helpful when it's triggered by mental stress.

Understanding what's happening in our bodies allows us to recognise the stress and use calming techniques to reset the response, helping us regain a sense of control and peace.

#45 Tip

Focus on how you want things to be.

By visualising a positive outcome, you can guide your thoughts in a direction that supports your well-being and goals, rather than letting worries or uncertainties take over.

This mindset helps create a sense of control and empowers you to navigate challenges with a clearer, more positive outlook.

#46 Tip

Remember, there is no such thing as failure,
only feedback.

If you find that something isn't working - whether it's
meditation or any other practice - that's perfectly okay!

Instead of seeing it as a setback, ask yourself what you
can learn from the experience or what you could
do differently.

Then, give it another go with a fresh perspective!

Every attempt is a step forward in your journey.

#47 Tip

If you're feeling stressed, ask yourself whether it stems from a lack of information, a loss of control, uncertainty - or all three.

Then consider what steps you can take to address each element.

Use the tools outlined in this book to guide you and take the necessary positive action.

CHAPTER 15 - WHY WORRY DOESN'T WORK

When we worry about the future, it's often not the things we're actually worried about that catch us off guard - it's the unexpected things, like receiving a cancer diagnosis at 50, that can really throw us off course. The truth is, worrying and doubting aren't really helping us prepare for the future. They are just draining our energy and keeping us stuck in a loop of uncertainty.

Worry or anxiety is usually caused by some or all of the following:

- Uncertainty about what's ahead.

- Lack of resources or support.

- Unrealistic expectations that set us up for disappointment.

- Unhelpful interpretations of the situation.

- Thinking that the problem is everywhere, forever, and your fault.

- Holding on to unhelpful beliefs about the situation.

The good news is, by recognising and managing these factors, you can start to shift from a place of worry to a place of mental resilience. It's all about making the choice to change how you respond. To help you along the way, here's a simple model to bring together some of the tips and tools we've covered throughout this book. With a little practice, you can move from anxiety to calm and start building your resilience for whatever life brings your way.

Uncertainty

One of the best ways to tackle uncertainty is to be prepared and plan for the practical things you might need. I found myself creating plan A, B, and C - once I worked through these in my mind, I felt a lot more at ease. It was like having the safety net there without needing to dwell on it. I knew I had it covered, and I could metaphorically leave those plans on the shelf, ready for whenever I might need them. This allowed me to focus more on moving forward and healing.

A big part of that was working on cultivating a positive mindset and reinforcing the beliefs that would support me through this challenging time. It's also so helpful to surround yourself with people who will do the same - people who lift you up, encourage you, or just offer a listening ear when needed.

Another great way to deal with uncertainty is by focusing on what you *can* control, instead of stressing over what's out of your hands. For example, you can't control what the surgeon says, how others will react, or waiting times but you *can* control:

- Your emotions.

- What you eat.

- Who you talk to.

- How much rest you get.

- The exercise you do.

- What you watch on TV.

- What you read.

So many things are within our control! Sometimes we just forget this. By focusing on the things that are within our control, we create a greater sense of certainty and stability in our lives.

Lack of resources

If you are feeling like you don't have the resources to handle whatever you are anxious or worried about, take some time to create resource anchors that will help you handle whatever comes your way. It's like preparing your toolkit in advance, so you've got everything ready when you need it.

Some of the most important resources you might need during this time are things like hope, calm, peace, and confidence. Spend some time thinking about what specific resources would help you the most and check out the tools section for ways to implement them.

One of the most critical resources I found I needed was flexibility. When things don't go as planned, having the flexibility to adapt is key. I learnt this pretty early on - my expectations and the reality of meetings or surgery results didn't always match up.

The first time this happened, it did shake my confidence in the system, but I made a conscious choice to change my attitude. By embracing flexibility, I was able to move forward more easily. I made extra plans (like I mentioned in the uncertainty section) and applied them as needed. I also worked on loosening my expectations, which made it much easier to roll with the changes.

Unrealistic expectations

I ran into this a lot during my journey - expecting that surgeries would be a precise science, or that I'd get my results exactly when I anticipated. The reality is, we can't change certain things that are outside of our control.

What I found incredibly helpful was lowering my expectations a bit and being flexible enough to deal with things that didn't go according to plan. This way, I wasn't as disappointed or caught off guard when setbacks or surprises came up. I learnt to take a realistic, yet still positive, view of the situation.

If we expect the world to be perfect, we're bound to feel disappointed. However, if we can accept that life is ever-changing and that we have the flexibility to adapt, it becomes much easier to cope.

This shift in attitude can make a huge difference in how we recover and navigate tough times. I touch on this in my book *Who's Flying Your Plane? How to master the controls of your life,* when I talk about the pessimist and optimist journey through life. Both can face the same ups and downs, but the optimist enjoys the highs for longer and spends less time in the lows, because they trust things will get better. The pessimist, on the other hand, tends to worry that the good times won't last, so they miss out on fully enjoying them. And when things do dip, they often say, 'I knew it wouldn't last', spending even more time in the tough moments. Both are going through the same events; however, their attitude toward them is what makes all the difference.

A great way to start shifting your perspective and becoming more optimistic is through gratitude. Check out Chapter 17 for ways to practise it in your life.

Unhelpful **interpretations**

I decided to reframe the situation to ... 'it will be what it will be'. This served me really well - it was less emotional than thinking, 'this is awful, I feel sorry for myself, this is terrible', and it was more realistic than telling myself, 'Everything is perfect', when that clearly wasn't the case. That neutral meaning allowed me to move forward more easily.

Now, that doesn't mean I didn't have moments of doubt or wobbles - I definitely did. However, over time, they became fewer and further between, and they stopped dominating my life. It's amazing how we can adapt to challenges over time.

Not me, not everywhere, not forever

I also love the idea that Michael Hall talks about in his book *Resilience: Being the Phoenix* (2020, p94, Figure 10.5). He suggests the concept of '*not me*, *not* everywhere, *not* forever'. It's a powerful way to remind yourself that no challenge is permanent or all-encompassing.

The 'not me' part is all about not taking things personally - remember back to the 'Why me?' chapter. Cancer isn't something that's targeted at you personally. Instead of beating ourselves up over what we may or may not have done to cause it, we can think of it as 'not me' (as in, it's not part of our identity, not who we are). It's not your fault; it's just something that's happening in this moment. Michael Hall's concept really helps us separate what happens to us from who we are as human beings.

You might recall that I talked about Event + Response = Outcome. This fits perfectly with that idea. The event - whether it's cancer or anything else - may not be something we can control or prevent. However, what we do control is our response to it. We have the power to decide how we think, how we act, and what meaning we attach to it. Being in the driver's seat of your own life means asking questions, seeking the information you need, and taking responsibility for how you move through it, rather than sitting back and accepting what happens to you.

I know that for some people, it's not easy to ask questions of medical professionals, for all kinds of reasons - fear, worry about looking foolish, or feeling like they are taking up their time. However, remember, this is your life, your body, and your health. You need to arm yourself with as much information as possible, so you can understand what's happening and take control of your own recovery. If you are feeling hesitant, the belief section can help you break through those mental blocks, and you can even create a resource anchor of confidence or courage to help you ask those tough questions.

Medical practitioners are just people like the rest of us, and it's part of their job to give us the information we need to recover. By asking questions, you are not only helping yourself; you are also helping them do their job better. I remember my second appointment with my surgeon - I came in with pages of questions. My final question was, 'Is there anything else I should have asked but haven't?' It's a great way to make sure you've covered all your bases. By doing this, you are being proactive and taking charge, instead of just being a passive bystander in the process.

Even in the midst of everything, we still have control over our thoughts and feelings. We still have choices - and that's something cancer can't take away from us. By making conscious, positive choices around our beliefs, emotions, and the meanings we assign to things, we can influence the outcome, especially in terms of how we feel about that outcome. And, let's face it, how we feel about the outcome is incredibly important.

The 'not everywhere' concept is also a valuable one to hold on to, especially if cancer has spread. It's easy to think that it's everywhere when the reality is, it's not. Even if it's spread widely, it's not technically everywhere. Keeping this in mind can help reduce the enormity of the situation. Remember my friend who said that it's only a few cells, out of the trillions we have in our body, that are affected. This really helped me mentally shrink the problem.

The 'not forever' part is incredibly helpful as well. In NLP, we talk about 'chunking down', which means breaking a situation into smaller, more manageable pieces. The surgery, the recovery, the treatment - it won't last forever. Neither will the pain, loss, or grief. Remembering this can help put things into perspective and give us the mental strength to keep moving forward, building resilience as we go.

Unhelpful beliefs

I made a conscious decision to upgrade my beliefs, choosing ones that were more supportive of my situation. The truth is, I didn't, and still don't, know what the future holds for me - none of us can predict that. However, I chose to shift away from unhelpful beliefs about my health and healing, and instead focused on positive, supportive ones. Whether they are true or not isn't the issue; what really matters is the impact they have on my mental well-being.

The same applies to you. Ultimately, you are in control of what you believe - provided that belief is doing no harm to you or others, and it's supporting your well-being, then holding positive beliefs about healing can only benefit you.

You've already taken steps to prepare, and with the knowledge you've gained, you now have a strategy to apply if you need it:

1. Plan for both the physical and emotional aspects, including 'just in case' options.

2. Access the resources you need, like calm and flexibility via your resource anchor.

3. Adjust your attitude by setting realistic expectations and focusing on gratitude.

4. Change the meaning you give to the situation so you can feel better using reframing.

5. Ensure your beliefs support you and change any that aren't working for you.

#48 Tip

It's often not the things we spend most of our time worrying about that cause the real problems.

It's usually the unexpected challenges that sneak up on us.

So instead of letting your energy go into worrying, focus on something more productive and empowering.

CHAPTER 16 - THE WRONG AVOCADO

An odd title for a chapter and book, I know! However, let me explain. It was after my third operation, and I was still waiting for the results. A few things happened all at once - I found out I needed significant dental work, and other health issues started to surface. I was still recovering from the third operation in six months, and I quickly realised I was feeling less resourceful than I needed to be.

One morning, as my husband was preparing breakfast, he cut, in my opinion, the *wrong* avocado! My reaction was ... extreme, to say the least. I became really angry at first, then hugely upset. Now, just to be clear, it wasn't actually about the avocado. I mean, I like them, but not to that extent!

So, what was really going on here?

We all have a metaphorical 'stress bucket' and my 'stress bucket' had overflowed! In modern life, there are so many things that can cause us stress: financial worries, work pressures, health concerns - the list goes on. All these things can get added to the bucket and we need to find a way to regularly empty it or at least keep the levels manageable. In other words, we need to prioritise self-care. That means practising things like meditation, mindfulness, eating healthily, getting enough sleep, nurturing good relationships with people we can talk to, and carving out time for relaxation and recovery. These are all essential for maintaining balance and resilience.

If we don't take the time to empty our stress buckets, they can fill up without us even realising it. My stress bucket had filled up with the news that I had cancer, the fact that two operations hadn't gone as planned, the ongoing uncertainty about whether the third operation would be successful, my other health and dental issues ... and then, of course, the avocado!

You've probably heard the phrase, 'the straw that broke the camel's back'. That's exactly what happened. The avocado was the final thing that caused my stress bucket to overflow ... and with it, all the emotions I had been holding back came flooding out, in tears.

It's so important to understand what you personally need to recharge. For my first two operations, I had the opportunity to get away for a week beforehand to be by water, relax, and really focus on emptying my stress bucket. However, for the third operation, I had less than a week's notice, and there were still so many unanswered questions. On top of that, I had a lot to sort out with my business, which meant I didn't get the chance to properly clear my head and reduce my stress before the operation. That's why, when the avocado incident happened, it was that 'straw that broke the camel's back' moment - the small thing that tipped me over the edge.

So, what can we do about it? Well, rather than waiting for the stress to overflow like I did, take the time now to think about what *you* need. Recognise when you are starting to feel stressed and take proactive steps to reduce it. Whether it's going for walks in nature, chatting with friends, or simply taking time to relax - whatever works for you, make sure you are doing it regularly to keep your stress levels in check. It's all about knowing yourself and finding what helps you feel centred and calm before things reach their breaking point.

Crying and hugging my husband was exactly what I needed in that moment. Along with that, I took a weekend off from working - something I desperately needed. For a couple of days, I didn't reply to any emails or do any work at all.

I gave myself the space to just *be* - no pressure, no expectations, just time to recharge. It's amazing how stepping away for a while can give you the clarity and relief you need to reset. Sometimes, we just need to give ourselves permission to pause and take care of our emotional well-being.

If you would like to explore self-care further, take a look at my book *Who's Flying Your Plane? How to master the controls of your life*.

#49 Tip

Recognise when your stress bucket is becoming full and take some time to look after yourself and empty it!

It's so important to check in with yourself regularly.

When life feels like it's piling up, make sure to take breaks, practise self-care, and find ways to unload some of that built-up stress.

Whether it's through a walk, a chat with a friend, or just taking a moment for yourself, emptying your stress bucket before it overflows can make a huge difference in how you feel and handle life's challenges.

CHAPTER 17 - TOOLS

In this chapter, I'll be sharing some tools that helped me through this journey, and that you can use too.

Note: If you'd like extra support, an NLP professional can help guide you through all these processes and other tools for even deeper transformation.

If you're listening to the audio version or joining in with the activities, just make sure you're somewhere safe and able to give them your full attention - so, not while driving or operating machinery.

Reframing

One of the most powerful tools I used during this time is reframing. Reframing helps you shift the meaning and interpretation you give to a situation. The reason it's so effective is simple: the meaning we assign to events directly influences how we feel about them.

For example, if you label a situation as 'bad', you are more likely to feel bad about it. If you think of it as 'sad', you will likely feel sad. But here's the great part - by choosing to see the situation as an opportunity, you can feel more optimistic, even in tough times. It's all about shifting your perspective to find a meaning that empowers you.

Reframing doesn't necessarily change the situation, but it does change how you feel about it. And when you feel more resourceful, you are better equipped to handle whatever comes your way.

To use this tool effectively, ask yourself, 'What else could this situation mean?' Keep asking that question until you come up with a variety of options that feel more helpful and useful to you. Once you have a few alternative meanings, you can then begin to rethink and change the narrative you are telling yourself about the situation.

This new narrative will be aligned with the more empowering meanings you've identified. It's about shifting your self-talk to reflect a perspective that supports your well-being and helps you move forward with a positive outlook. This simple question can truly transform the way you experience challenges, helping you feel more in control.

Further explanation

Imagine you're driving and someone suddenly cuts you up, speeding past and weaving in front of you. In that moment, you have a choice in how you interpret the situation. One option might be to assume they're being rude or inconsiderate - and if you go with that meaning, you may notice feelings like frustration, agitation, or even anger starting to bubble up.

But this is where reframing comes in. Reframing invites us to pause and ask, 'What else might this mean?' After all, we don't truly know the reason behind their behaviour. Maybe they're running late for an important appointment. Perhaps they've just had some upsetting news, or they're rushing to the hospital to see a loved one or trying to help in an emergency.

Any of these possibilities could be just as true as your first assumption - we simply don't know.

If you're anything like me, these alternative meanings tend to bring up very different emotions: perhaps compassion, empathy, or even a moment of kindness. When we don't have all the facts, our minds can fill in the blanks - we begin mindreading. So, if we're going to mindread anyway, why not choose a version that feels better? One that supports us emotionally, instead of dragging us down.

Reframing doesn't mean denying reality - it simply means giving yourself the gift of another perspective. A perspective that might just leave you feeling more at ease.

Energy clearing

Clearing energy from others is a great tool when you've absorbed the energy or emotions of those around you. This process helps to realign and restore your own energy, leaving you feeling more centred and balanced. Here's how you can do it:

1. Take a moment to get comfortable and close your eyes.

2. Pay attention to any energy you are holding that doesn't belong to you. Notice where this energy is in or around you.

3. Visualise sending this foreign energy to the centre of the earth for recycling.

4. Continue noticing and sending away any energy that isn't yours. Do this until you feel clear of any external influences.

5. Once you've let go of others' energy, take a moment to reconnect with your own. Feel your personal energy building up inside you - pure, clean, and revitalising - and let it flow through your body.

6. Slowly open your eyes and notice how you feel now - more grounded, balanced, and aligned with your own energy.

This technique can be incredibly helpful when you've been around others who may be carrying heavy emotions or energy that doesn't serve you.

Further explanation

It's a bit like using a magnet to pick up metal objects. Sometimes we attract exactly what we intended - things that are useful or meaningful to us. But other times, we pick up bits and pieces we didn't mean to collect - unwanted thoughts, habits, or emotions that have simply stuck to us along the way.

This process gives us the chance to gently sort through what we've gathered. We can choose to let go of what no longer serves us, keeping hold of only what we truly want to carry forward.

How to access your inner resources: creating a resource anchor

Creating a resource anchor is a powerful way to tap into your inner strength whenever you need it - whether it's before surgery or during any challenging situation. I recommend creating your anchor in advance so that it's ready to use whenever you need it. By preparing ahead of time, you can easily access the calm, confidence, or the emotion you need to feel supported, no matter what you are facing.

What emotional states do you think you will need? When I created my own anchor, I focused on calm, feeling grounded, flexibility, and confidence. These are the emotional states that really helped me during challenging moments.

One great way to create this connection is through a kinaesthetic anchor. This means you can trigger a positive emotional response, like confidence or calm, with just the press of your finger using neuroplasticity to create a new neurological pathway. It teaches your brain to automatically respond to a specific trigger.

The process works through classic conditioning i.e. repeating something several times to strengthen the neurological pathway. Essentially, you repeat the action; pressing your knuckle for example, while you are feeling that desired emotional state. Over time, your brain forms a new link between that trigger (the touch on your knuckle) and the emotional response (like confidence).

By practising this in advance, you are setting up that neurological pathway, so when you press your trigger later, you will instantly feel that emotion you've anchored. It's like a shortcut to your best self in the moment.

1. Before you begin, make sure that you are comfortable with having this new emotion available to you whenever you need it. It's important to feel good about the changes you are making.

2. Pick a spot that's easy to press and feels natural - your knuckle, for example. It should be somewhere discreet, so you can easily press it when you need to, without drawing attention.

3. Think back to a specific moment when you felt this emotion strongly. Really step into that memory - see what you saw, hear what you heard, and notice how you felt. Feel those emotions again, right now. Pay attention to how you stood, how you breathed, and what you said to yourself in that moment. Once you are feeling it, imagine a dial from 1 to 10, where 1 is a low intensity and 10 is the strongest. Notice where you are on the dial, and then slowly turn it up, bringing the feeling to about an 8, making it stronger with every breath.

4. When the feeling reaches around 8, press your knuckle (or where you have decided to create your anchor) and hold it for approximately 15 seconds. As you do, let the feeling intensify until it's almost

at its maximum - just before it hits 10. Then, remove your finger.

5. Repeat steps 3 and 4 several times. The more you repeat this process, the stronger the neurological pathway becomes. Each time you do it, the connection between your trigger (the knuckle press) and the emotional response gets more powerful. It's like wiring your brain to respond automatically in the way you want.

6. After you've done this a few times, take a break to do something else. Then, press your knuckle and see how quickly those feelings come back. If you would like the feeling to be even stronger, simply repeat the process until it's as powerful as you want it to be.

Now, whenever you want to feel that emotion, all you have to do is press your knuckle. It's similar to how just looking at or smelling your favourite food can make you feel good - it's an automatic response. By firing your anchor, you instantly tap into the emotional state you've created.

Essentially, you've formed a new 'stimulus-response' connection: a trigger (pressing your knuckle) that brings up an unconscious emotional response.

You can repeat this process for the other emotional states you want to access. You can even stack multiple anchors in the same spot, so that with one press, you can experience a range of feelings when you need them most. To do this, just repeat the process with each new state you want using the same trigger and testing each as you go.

Further explanation

We create resource anchors all the time - often without even realising it. Think about a moment when you've smelled your favourite meal. Chances are, it brought back memories filled with positive emotions. Or perhaps you heard a favourite piece of music and instantly felt uplifted. Maybe you saw a picture of a cute animal and felt a wave of love. These are all examples of naturally occurring anchors - sensory triggers that connect to emotional states.

In the process I've just shared with you, we're simply taking that natural, unconscious mechanism and using it consciously. We're creating a new anchor on purpose, using the power of neuroplasticity - our brain's ability to rewire itself by forming new connections.

Here's how it works: when you hear a song you love - that sound acts as a trigger. A specific neural pathway fires, and you feel good. In this exercise, we're doing something similar, but instead of using music, we're linking those positive feelings to something simple and accessible - like pressing a knuckle. Over time, your brain learns to associate that physical action with the good feeling you've anchored to it.

If it feels easier for you, you can absolutely use music or another meaningful trigger - like imagining your favourite song in your mind. The effect is the same.

What's beautiful about this tool is that it gives you choice. You don't have to wait for a good moment to come along and lift your mood - you can gently create it, whenever you need it.

Removing unwanted emotions: Collapsing Anchors

This technique helps you get rid of unwanted emotions such as anxiety about scans, operations or treatments, by using the same principles as the resource anchor. Essentially, it works by cancelling out the unwanted emotion - like a chemistry experiment from your school days, where you add alkaline to acid until it becomes neutral. In this case, you are using a positive anchor to shift the emotional response, and from a neurological perspective, it neutralises the unwanted emotion.

It's a simple but powerful way to take control of your emotional state and create a more balanced, positive experience.

1. Before you begin, make sure you are truly ready to release this unwanted emotion. Take a moment to check what you might gain or lose by making this change and ensure that the consequences feel okay for you.

2. Choose which knee you'd like to use for this step - let's say your left knee. Now, think about the trigger that brings up the unwanted emotion. Once you start feeling it, press your left knee for about 5 seconds. This anchors that unwanted emotion to your left knee.

3. Take a minute to think about something that makes you feel good - something you truly love to do. Let the positive feelings from that memory fill you up.

4. Next, think about some positive, strong emotions that you can easily access - like confidence, joy, or happiness. These are your resource states, the ones that feel uplifting and good for you.

5. Now, use your other knee (e.g., right knee) to anchor each of these positive emotions individually. Follow the resource anchor technique from earlier in the chapter, pressing your right knee each time you feel each of the strong emotions you want to anchor, holding it for 15

seconds. Repeat as necessary and test each anchor by pressing your knee as you go. Make sure you are pressing the exact same spot on your right knee each time.

6. Once you've anchored all the positive states, press your right knee and see how strong those feelings are. They should feel much stronger than the unwanted emotion on your left knee. If they don't yet, repeat the anchoring process until they feel significantly stronger.

7. Pause and think about something light and neutral - maybe your favourite movie, for example. Just take a mental break before moving on.

8. Now, it's time to collapse the anchors! Press your left knee (where the unwanted emotion is anchored) and hold it. Then, press your right knee (where the positive emotions are anchored). Hold both knees for a few minutes, letting the positive emotions neutralise the unwanted one. You might feel some tingling, fizzing, or a flow of energy - any

of that is perfectly fine. When it feels complete, remove your finger from your left knee (the unwanted emotion), then leave your right knee pressed for another 5 seconds before removing your finger from there as well.

9. Now, ask yourself how you feel about that old unwanted emotion. Notice how your relationship to that feeling has shifted.

10. Finally, think a time in the future when you might face a similar situation to the one where you experienced that unwanted emotion. Notice what happens now - how do you respond to the situation with your new more neutral perspective?

Changing limiting beliefs

The process we are about to explore will help you go back to the very first time you (unconsciously) created a limiting belief. By doing this, you can shift it at its root and create a more empowering belief instead.

To do this, we will use something called a timeline. We all have an internal timeline - it's how we mentally organise time. Think about it; you instinctively know the difference between yesterday and tomorrow because you store those memories and thoughts differently in your mind. Without this internal timeline, everything would feel jumbled!

In this process, you will use your timeline to revisit the moment that belief was formed, giving you the chance to release it and replace it with something far more useful.

Discovering your timeline

Before we begin shifting limiting beliefs, let's first explore how you mentally organise time.

1. Close your eyes and think about something you did last year. As you recall this memory, notice where it feels like it exists in relation to you. Does it seem to be in front of you? To the side? Behind you? Above or below? There's no right or wrong answer - just observe where it naturally appears.

2. Close your eyes again and think about something you are planning to do next year. Pay attention to where this thought is positioned. Is it in front of you? To the left or right? Behind you? Somewhere else? Just like before, there's no correct answer - just notice what comes up.

3. Shift your focus to the here and now. Where do you perceive the present moment in relation to you?

4. Now that you've identified these three locations - your past, your present, and your future - imagine drawing a line that connects them. This is what we call your timeline. It's your personal mental map of time, and we'll use it to help shift limiting beliefs at their core.

Take a moment to visualise this timeline. Notice its direction and how it feels to see time laid out in this way. Once you have a sense of your timeline, you are ready for the next step!

Further explanation

Timeline is a metaphor for how we organise time in our minds. It's widely used in project and change management, and here, we're using it in a similar way - to explore your personal timeline, from past experiences, through the present, and into your future plans.

It's a helpful tool because it allows you to take a step back and look at your life with greater perspective - gathering insight, learning, and wisdom from everything you've already lived through.

In this next exercise, we use your timeline to help shift beliefs that may be holding you back.

Beliefs are like personal truths - things we consciously or unconsciously hold to be true about ourselves or the world around us. We can begin to uncover them simply by listening in on our internal dialogue. What are you saying to yourself? It might be something like: 'I'll never get better,' or 'I always knew I would end up unwell.'

While it's important to acknowledge difficult thoughts, it's equally important to hold beliefs that support and nurture us. That doesn't mean being in denial - it simply means recognising that we don't always know what's ahead, and that our beliefs aren't always facts. Often, we make predictions about our future based on what's happened in the past.

The good news is, we can change our beliefs. In fact, we already do this naturally throughout life. For example, as a child, you may have believed wholeheartedly in Father Christmas. And then one day, something happened - a moment that changed your view. Perhaps you saw a parent putting presents under the tree, or you overheard a conversation, and in that instant, your belief shifted.

We're simply using that same natural process here but doing it consciously and with intention. Instead of waiting for a belief to shift on its own, we gently guide the process using this timeline technique - giving ourselves the power to let go of what no longer serves us, and to create new beliefs that support our wellbeing and growth.

For instance, I used this process to shift a deeply ingrained belief I held after losing members of my family to cancer. I had unconsciously assumed the same would happen to me. But I came to realise that belief wasn't a fact, and I had the choice to change it.

Releasing limiting beliefs using your timeline

Now that you've connected with your timeline, let's use it to transform an old limiting belief - one that has been holding you back.

This process will take you back to the very first time this belief was created. Even if you don't consciously remember when it happened, your unconscious mind does. By revisiting that moment with the wisdom and perspective you have today, you can uncover new insights, shift your understanding, and replace the old belief with one that truly serves you.

1. Before we begin, take a moment to check in with yourself. Is it okay to release this belief today? What will be different in your life once it's gone? Are you ready to step into a new way of thinking?

2. When you are ready, close your eyes and take a few deep gentle breaths.

3. Imagine yourself gently lifting up above your timeline, so you can see the past stretching in one direction and the future extending in the other. You are observing it all from a safe, comfortable space.

4. Now, trust your unconscious mind and allow yourself to float back along your timeline to the very first time this limiting belief was formed. Even if you don't recall a specific event, you may get a feeling or an image when you arrive. As you float above this moment, imagine yourself inside a clear protective bubble - you are safe and supported.

5. Looking down from this safe space, ask your unconscious mind: 'What positive learnings can I take from this event?'

    Now, with the wisdom of your adult self, observe what was happening to the younger you in that moment.

Some insights may include:

- I was just a child, doing my best with what I knew at the time.

- The expectations placed on me were unrealistic.

- This situation didn't mean what I thought it did.

- I misunderstood what was happening.

Let your unconscious mind reveal the lessons that will allow you to move forward.

6. Ask yourself: 'Is there anything else I need to learn?' If so, take a moment to absorb those insights.

7. If you could step into this moment and give advice to your younger self, what would you say? Offer reassurance and encouragement.

8. Reassure your unconscious mind that these valuable learnings will always be available when needed. Your mind's highest priority is to protect you, and once it feels safe, it will allow you to let go.

9. Notice what resources your younger self needs - for example, love, courage, or wisdom. Anchor these resources using the resource anchor technique mentioned earlier in the chapter.

10. Now fire (press) your anchor, and imagine stepping into that past moment - this time with all the resources, insights, and wisdom you have now. Notice how different it feels. If any old emotions or limiting beliefs remain, simply float back up and ask: 'What else do I need to learn?' Once you have the answer, float into the event again and see how it shifts.

11. Ask yourself: 'What do I believe now?' Notice how your perspective has changed.

12. Once it feels complete, float back up above and before the event, fire (press) your anchor again, and begin moving forward along your timeline, noticing how the new belief ripples through every experience that followed. Observe how past situations now look different in light of what you've learnt.

13. Now, float forward into the future and visit a specific situation where, in the past, you would have had the old belief. Notice how different it feels now.

    Next, move to a second future event and observe how your new belief transforms that situation.

    Finally, visit a third event even further in the future - fully experiencing your incredible, empowering new belief.

14. Once you've explored these future moments, float back to the present and gently return to the room.

Now, ask yourself: 'What do I believe now?'

Notice how different it feels - how much lighter, clearer, and more empowered you are.

You have just rewritten the meaning of an old story and replaced it with one that supports you.

This is the power of your mind, and this is how transformation happens.

If you find it easier, record yourself reading these steps aloud and then listen back as you guide yourself through the process.

Alternatively, you can simply read one step at a time, close your eyes, and complete it before moving on - both methods work well.

Gratitude

Practising gratitude is one of the simplest yet most powerful things you can do. You can keep a gratitude journal and write down what you are thankful for or simply take a moment each day to list them in your mind.

Start by thinking of ten new things you are grateful for each day - and as you build this habit, you will find even more to appreciate. Once you have written your list or reflected on each one, pause and truly feel that gratitude. Let the feeling grow, expand, and flow through your entire body. Notice how good it feels to embrace gratitude.

The more you practise, the more joy and positivity you will invite into your life.

Further explanation

Practising gratitude is like adjusting the brightness on your television. It doesn't change the picture itself; however, it does help you see the brighter parts more clearly.

If life feels heavy or overwhelming, especially during difficult times, everything can seem a little dim. But by gently focusing on what we're grateful for, no matter how small, we begin to notice things we may have overlooked. A kind word, a sunny day or a beautiful smile.

Gratitude doesn't erase the challenges; however, it can soften them. It brings a sense of balance and brightness, helping us to see more clearly even when the picture isn't perfect.

Breathing techniques

These are wonderfully simple yet powerful ways to help you feel calm and balanced.

Balanced Breathing involves inhaling gently and slowly for the same count as you exhale - for example, breathing in for a count of 4 and out for a count of 4. This naturally helps to settle your nervous system and bring a sense of ease.

You can also do Box Breathing, a simple yet effective technique to calm the nervous system. It involves four equal steps:

1. Breathe in for a count of 4.

2. Hold for a count of 4.

3. Breathe out for a count of 4.

4. And hold again for a count of 4.

5. Then repeat the cycle.

Alternatively, if you want to deeply relax - perhaps to ease pain or drift off to sleep - try extending your exhale. Breathe in for a count of 4 and out for a count of 6 (or even longer if it feels comfortable). The longer exhale signals to your body that it's safe to relax, helping you feel even more at peace. Give it a go and notice how quickly your body responds.

Further explanation

These breathing techniques are a bit like rebooting your computer. When things feel overloaded or stuck, a reset helps everything run more smoothly. In the same way, conscious breathing helps to calm the nervous system, quiet the mind, and restore balance - so you can move forward with greater clarity and resourcefulness.

The great thing is, you can do this at anytime, anywhere without anyone noticing - no fancy equipment needed!

Grounding technique

This is a wonderful tool to help you feel more centred if life feels a little out of control. There are many ways to feel more grounded, and this is one of my favourites:

1. Find a comfortable position, either sitting or standing, with both feet firmly on the floor.

2. Think of something you are really good at or something you love doing. Spend a moment fully immersing yourself in that experience - notice what you see, hear, and feel when you are engaged in it.

3. Now, bring in a colour - any colour that feels good to you and represents that feeling of confidence and joy.

4. Fill yourself with that colour - let it flow through your body, all the way down into your toes.

5. Imagine the colour flowing out through your feet, like the roots of a tree, spreading wide and deep into the earth.

6. Let those roots support you. Feel that deep connection to the ground beneath you, knowing you are safe, steady, and grounded.

7. Take a deep gentle breath and enjoy the feeling of stability and strength flowing through you.

Further explanation

Did you know that an oak tree's roots can spread underground just as far as its branches reach into the sky? This deep and wide root system gives the tree its stability. When strong winds blow or storms roll in, the branches may bend and some leaves may be lost, but the tree still stands.

Grounding works in much the same way for us. It helps us stay rooted when life feels turbulent. It doesn't mean we won't sway or feel the effects of the storm, but it gives us the inner strength to remain standing.

Taking the time to develop a sense of being grounded using the exercise above helps to build resilience, especially during times of deep uncertainty or emotional upheaval, like facing cancer.

New Behaviour Generator (visualisation)

This technique helps you mentally rehearse a new behaviour, allowing you to step into a situation fully prepared and confident. Whether it's a difficult conversation, or a personal challenge, this process creates new neurological pathways, so your desired response becomes second nature.

1. Before making a change, ask yourself: 'Will the consequences of this change be positive in all areas of my life? Does this new behaviour align with my values and goals?' If you have answered 'yes' to both questions, continue to the next step.

2. Close your eyes and imagine yourself as a movie director of your own life. See the scene in front of you, playing out the situation you want to change. Observe yourself in this scene.

3. Watch the scene unfold with your new behaviour in place - calm, poised, and effective. Make any

adjustments until it plays out exactly as you would like.

4. Now, step into the movie and replay the situation, but this time, see it through your own eyes. Notice how it feels to embody this new behaviour. Observe the positive ripple effect - how others respond, the energy in the room, and how natural it all feels. Ask yourself: Does this feel right? If not, go back to the director's chair and refine it.

5. Replay the scene multiple times, both as the director and as yourself inside the scene. Each repetition strengthens the neurological pathway, making it feel more natural. If relevant, practise additional scenarios - for example, receiving unexpected information in a meeting with your consultant and notice how you manage that with ease and confidence.

6. Once you are happy with it, open your eyes. Think about a future time when you may need to display that new behaviour and notice how easy it is to do.

Further explanation

By rehearsing a new behaviour in your mind, you may notice a sense of déjà vu when you face the real situation because your mind and body already know how to respond.

It's a bit like learning to ride a bike - at first, it might feel a little wobbly or uncertain. But with practice, you become steadier, more confident, and a more natural rider.

This tool allows you to mentally practise something you want to do before you actually do it. That way, when the real moment arrives, it feels more familiar. You've already begun to build the neurological pathways for the new behaviour, making it easier to access in real time.

You can use this approach in all sorts of situations; from breaking an old habit to preparing for a difficult conversation. It's a gentle, effective way to build confidence and create change.

CHAPTER 18 - ADDITIONAL SUPPORT

I trust this book has given you some simple yet powerful tools to help make your journey a little easier. As I often say, NLP won't create a perfect life - but it can help you meet its challenges with greater ease and resilience.

While it may not take away your cancer or health condition, it can guide you through the emotional journey, helping you feel stronger, more resilient, and better equipped to face each day with greater peace and confidence. I know this to be true - because I've used these very tools (and many more) on my own healing journey, and they changed everything.

Your journey is deeply personal. I hope some of the ideas and techniques I've shared have resonated with you and supported you along the way.

If you feel you'd benefit from one-to-one coaching to help navigate any current challenges, I'd love to support you

further. You're very welcome to reach out via my website:
www.achieveyourgreatness.co.uk

Explore NLP further

If you'd like to dive deeper into NLP and discover how it can help you live a more empowered and authentic life, I offer several courses (full details are on my website):

- **NLP Practitioner Training** - a comprehensive journey where you'll learn these and many more life-changing tools to support both yourself and others.

- **Identity By Design** - a short course that helps you uncover who you truly are at your core, beyond any labels (including 'cancer'), so you can create a life that reflects the *real* you.

- **Core Transformation** - a gentle yet powerful approach to inner change, healing, and growth (created by Connirae Andreas).

- **The Secret of Sleep** - Learn simple, effective techniques to calm your mind, break old habits, and enjoy deep, refreshing sleep.

Whether you're looking for personal development or feel called to help others, these courses are designed to give you lasting tools for transformation.

Additional avenues of support

You are not alone. There are so many people and organisations ready to support you:

- Lady McAdden Breast Cancer Trust: www.ladymcadden.org

- Macmillan Cancer Support: www.macmillan.org.uk

- Your local GP or cancer nurse specialist.

No question is too small. No feeling is too much. If you need help, *please* ask for it.

Throughout my own healing journey, I found regular Reiki sessions incredibly helpful in bringing peace and balance to my body and mind.

I also read widely - books became a source of hope, insight, and inspiration. If you're looking for valuable reading, here are a few I recommend:

- *Who's Flying Your Plane? How to master the controls of your life* (Emma R McNally MBA).

- *Resilience. Being the Phoenix* (L. Michael Hall, PhD, 2020).

- *How Your Mind Can Heal Your Body* (Dr David R Hamilton PhD).

Navigating nutrition

When it comes to nutrition, you'll likely find *a lot* of information out there - some of it helpful, some of it confusing, and some even contradictory. My advice?

Speak to a qualified nutritionist who understands your specific type of cancer and treatment.

People often mean well, but not everyone has the medical insight you may need. I discovered that certain medications can affect how your body absorbs vitamins, and that some foods are best avoided, or increased, depending on your treatment. Getting expert advice made a big difference for me, and it might for you too.

Feed your mind as well as your body

One of the most empowering things you can do is stay curious. Seek out information. Look for tools that help. My hunger for helpful, practical, uplifting knowledge played a fundamental role in helping me through.

In addition to reading, I found guided visualisations and meditations incredibly soothing and supportive throughout my healing. I listened to them regularly, especially when things felt uncertain or overwhelming.

Here are a few I wholeheartedly recommend:

- www.therobinsongroup.ca/the-secret-garden-guided-meditations/

- www.drdavidhamilton.com/howtovisualise

This chapter is titled 'Additional Support', but really - it's about reminding you that you don't have to do this alone. Whether through NLP, coaching, meditation, or the compassionate care of professionals and charities, there is help out there.

#50 Tip

Ask for help.

Remember, asking for help is a sign of strength,
not weakness.

Even if you are struggling to put into words exactly what
you need, reaching out is the first step.

There are so many people who genuinely want to
support you - so remember to ask.

If it's something that requires specialist knowledge, like
nutrition, be sure to seek guidance from a qualified
expert who understands your specific needs.

CHAPTER 19 - FINAL THOUGHTS

Thank you for taking the time to read this book. I truly hope that some of the tools shared help make this part of your life a little easier.

If you are reading this to better understand what a loved one is going through, I want to express my heartfelt gratitude to you. That kind of support is truly amazing and shows how much you care and makes a real difference.

For those who are curious, I am now two years post-surgery, and after my third operation - fourth lumpectomy - I received some unexpected news: my second tumour turned out to be benign.

Naturally, I had to double-check with my surgeon. The original biopsies clearly showed it was cancer, but by the time they finally removed it, it was benign.

So, once again, I found myself moving through the change curve, processing this twist in the journey, and using my

NLP tools to reframe the situation. There are a few possible explanations:

1. They removed all the cancer during the original biopsy - maybe, but unlikely as the needle was big, but not that big!

2. It was misdiagnosed from the start - possible, though the hospital doesn't agree with this theory.

3. They didn't remove the second cancer, and it is still there - unlikely, as multiple follow-up mammograms have come back clear.

4. Or ... my body healed itself. Whether through a natural process or the healing work I committed to, we'll never truly know.

I choose to believe in option 4, rather than dwell on the thought that I went through all of that for nothing. At the end of the day, it all comes down to choice. It took me time to reach this perspective, but shifting my mindset in this way serves me so much better moving forward.

As I've said before, everyone's journey is unique. You may not have had the same experiences as I did, but the tools shared in this book are adaptable. You can use them not only for your current situation but also for any other challenge life throws your way.

One of the most powerful things we can offer another human being is love and empathy. In my book *Who's Flying Your Plane? How to master the controls of your life*, I describe the difference between empathy and sympathy. Empathy is like throwing a rope down to someone, helping them climb out of a hole. Sympathy is jumping into the hole with them - so now *both* of you need rescuing!

Some of the most comforting moments for me were when people were just honest and said, 'I don't know what to say.' That kind of vulnerability was beautiful. It showed they cared.

If you're caring for someone going through illness, it's completely normal to feel many of the emotions described in this book. I know I did when my dad went through cancer. There's often a sense of helplessness - the longing to ease their pain, to make them well again - and the heartbreak of knowing that some things are simply out of our control.

Unfortunately, you can't do it *for* them. But you *can* be there for them. The emotional landscape can shift dramatically from day to day, so just be there. Ask what they need and offer your support with kindness.

You don't need to fix anything. They simply need your love.

Through my own experience, I've come to understand that the only person who can change my thinking is *me*. And the good news? That puts us back in charge of our lives. So, when you're ready, you *can* use the tools and ideas shared here to support your own journey, too.

There's so much more I could share, but I'll leave it here for now.

If you have any questions, or if you'd like to explore how NLP can help you navigate life's challenges, I'd be honoured to support you.

Sending you warm, healing energy, and remember - you've got this.

Emma x

ABOUT THE AUTHOR

Why NLP?

When I discovered NLP in 2010, it was like finding the missing piece of life's puzzle. Suddenly, everything made more sense - relationships, work, family, and most importantly, *myself.*

It completely transformed the way I viewed and responded to the world around me. Since then, NLP has become a part of who I am. It's shaped the way I navigate life's inevitable ups and downs, giving me a toolkit for resilience, clarity, and growth.

Sharing the secret

I'm passionate about sharing these incredible tools because, to me, it felt like I'd unlocked a secret - a way to live life with stronger relationships, greater success, and more control over my emotions, beliefs, and choices.

NLP didn't make life perfect. But it *did* give me the strength to face life's challenges and the insight to move forward with purpose.

We're all a work in progress. Learning how to steer your own course - rather than being tossed around by life's turbulence - can change everything.

That's why my mission is to make NLP accessible to as many people as possible, so they too can create a life that truly works for *them*.

My approach

Through my company, Achieve Your Greatness Ltd (School of NLP), I provide a safe and supportive space where people can explore who they truly are.

Whether you're looking to strengthen your mindset, navigate the emotional challenges of illness, support your recovery, or simply live a more fulfilled life, NLP offers powerful, practical tools to help you get there.

My approach focuses on helping you to take control of your mindset and use NLP techniques to support resilience, well-being, and help you thrive.

If you're ready to harness the power of your mind to enhance your health, happiness, and future - I'd love to support you on that journey.

Learn more at: www.achieveyourgreatness.co.uk

Or check out my other book: *Who's Flying Your Plane? How to master the controls of your life*

Printed in Dunstable, United Kingdom